Instructions

LET AUGMENTED REALITY CHANGE HOW YOU READ A BOOK

With your smartphone, iPad or tablet you can use the **Hasmark AR** app to invoke the augmented reality experience to literally read outside the book.

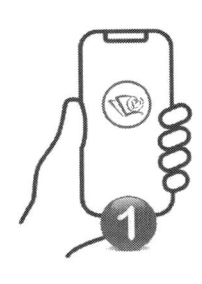

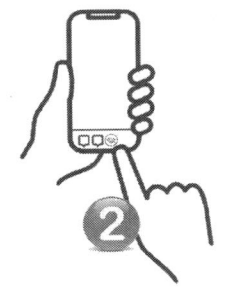

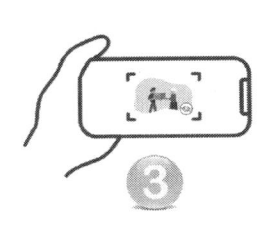

1. Download the **Hasmark app** from the **Apple App Store** or **Google Play**
2. Open and select the (vue) option
3. Point your lens at the full image with the and enjoy the augmented reality experience.

Go ahead and try it right now with the Hasmark Publishing International logo.

The River of Life

Endorsements

Hanne Buggild's book explores tragic themes of betrayal, abandonment, and abuse. In her book, she reveals an exceptional human spirit and the power of resilience and strength to overcome difficult circumstances.

—**Peggy McColl**,
New York Times Bestselling Author

The River of Life: Staying Afloat is a gripping book that captures the reader's attention from start to finish. Hannah's journey toward survival is so captivating that the reader becomes emotionally invested in her story. Follow her path, and find yourself willing her to break free from her past and thrive in a new life.

—**Judy O'Beirn**,
International Bestselling Author

The River of Life

Staying Afloat

HANNE BUGGILD

Hasmark
PUBLISHING
INTERNATIONAL

Published by
Hasmark Publishing International
www.hasmarkpublishing.com

Copyright © 2023 Hanne Buggild
First Edition

No part of this book may be reproduced or transmitted in any form or by any means, electronic or mechanical, including photocopying, recording or by any information storage and retrieval system, without written permission from the author, except for the inclusion of brief quotations in a review.

Disclaimer

This book is designed to provide information and motivation to our readers. It is sold with the understanding that the publisher is not engaged to render any type of psychological, legal, or any other kind of professional advice. The content of each article is the sole expression and opinion of its author, and not necessarily that of the publisher. No warranties or guarantees are expressed or implied by the publisher's choice to include any of the content in this volume. Neither the publisher nor the individual author(s) shall be liable for any physical, psychological, emotional, financial, or commercial damages, including, but not limited to, special, incidental, consequential or other damages. Our views and rights are the same: You are responsible for your own choices, actions, and results.

Permission should be addressed in writing to Hanne Buggild at support@hannebuggild.com

Editor: Deanna Novak deanna@hasmarkpublishing.com
Cover Designer: Anne Karklins anne@hasmarkpublishing.com
Layout Artist: Amit Dey amit@hasmarkpublishing.com

ISBN 13: 978-1-77482-215-9
ISBN 10: 1774822156

Dedication

To my three beloved sons and all the members of my Soul Family who made have my journey along the River of Life absolutely amazing.

Table of Contents

The River of Life xi

Prologue xi

Chapter 1 1

Chapter 2 11

Chapter 3 17

Chapter 4 25

Chapter 5 33

Chapter 6 47

Chapter 7 55

Chapter 8 67

Chapter 9 77

Chapter 10 87

Chapter 11 109

Chapter 12 123

Chapter 13 139

Chapter 14 147

Chapter 15 157

Chapter 16 167
Chapter 17 171
Chapter 18 191
Chapter 19 205
Chapter 20 217
Chapter 21 231
About the Author 237

The River of Life

Prologue

Hannah looked down into a shaft of darkness. The breast was far away. The shaft closed, and there was no breast, only darkness. A sharp, searing pain cut through her body, and she collapsed, clutching her stomach. Hannah touched her left breast and ran a hand over her stomach, trying to tell the child how sorry she was. She tried to explain to the child, who was no longer a child, that it was an accident, but the pain stopped her.

The river was dark, and the pain was constant, like a giant rock in the dark river. After what felt like a thousand years, there was a small glimpse of light in the dark.

A gentle female voice spoke in a loving tone that made Hannah feel safe. The soft voice kept talking. Part of the threatening darkness disappeared, and Hannah suddenly became aware that she was lying in a bed—a bed that was too short for her tall body—and that someone was holding her hand.

Hannah's whole body ached, and suddenly she remembered it all. Her thoughts rushed in like water cascading from a giant waterfall and she started sobbing uncontrollably.

Hannah's hysterical crying brought a nurse into the room. She was ready to intervene, but she seemed to quickly realize that the woman sitting at the bedside had complete control of the situation and left the room.

The woman was reaching over the bed and holding Hannah close to her breast, humming and caressing her long, curly, golden-brown hair.

Slowly Hannah calmed down. She blinked once more and managed to fully open her eyes. She turned toward the light and saw a middle-aged woman with black and gray-streaked hair, set up in a loose neck bun, sitting by her bed. An unknown woman.

"You've come back! Oh, thank God, you're back," the woman said.

Hannah tried to talk. "How long?" Her voice was only a whisper.

"Five days. You've been in the hospital for five days. But you must not speak; you must not speak at all."

Only five days? Then she was still only seventeen and not old enough to make her own decisions.

"Who are you?" Hannah's voice was so weak that the woman had to bend down and put an ear to her mouth to hear her.

"My name is Virginia," she said, smiling a warm, loving smile that made her face light up.

"But who ARE you?"

Virginia rose and tucked the blanket more snugly around Hannah's tall body without answering the question. Instead, she flicked a little fart and asked, "How tall are you, my sweet girl?"

"Six feet, four inches." Hannah tried to pull her legs further up under the duvet, but Virginia gently held her feet in place and began to massage them with light, calm movements, holding her gaze the whole time.

"No one has ever massaged my feet. It feels amazing!" Hannah relaxed and enjoyed the comfort of Virginia's gentle hands.

"A foot massage is one of the best ways to relax." Virginia looked thoughtfully at Hannah and asked, "Does being that tall bother you?"

Hannah nodded. "Yes, I hate being so unnaturally tall. It's ruined my life…" She began to cry uncontrollably again, feeling consumed by her misery.

"What nonsense, my sweet girl. It's not your height that makes the difference. It's your own thoughts about your height that need a little work."

Virginia released Hannah's feet and sat next to her on the bed. She started stroking Hannah's lovely golden-brown hair again, which, although it required a wash and a brush, gleamed beautifully in the soft glow of the small lamp by the bedside.

Hannah blinked her hazel eyes and tried to focus on the nice woman, but her eyes filled with tears.

Virginia gently wiped them away and kissed Hannah's hand. "Do your wounds hurt, my sweet girl?"

Virginia looked thoughtfully at the many cuts and scratches on the young girl's beautiful face and the thick bandage covering her breasts.

Hannah sobbed, "Yes, it hurts, but it doesn't matter. Nothing matters anymore…"

"Don't ever think like that. It's important to always think positive thoughts."

"But nobody cares about me. I'm all alone now…"

"What nonsense. I'm right here and I certainly do care for you."

"Why are you here? Do you know me?" Hannah did not understand why this stranger, although seemingly very nice, should care about her.

"No, my sweet girl, I don't know you. But I hope to get to know you soon." For a moment, Virginia's eyes wandered away from the young girl lying in bed to her own bag, where a folded newspaper was peeking out.

Hannah looked puzzled. "Why do you want to know me?"

"Don't worry about that right now—the important thing is that *you* get better."

"Do you live nearby?" Hannah wondered if Virginia was some kind of visiting friend who came to visit sick people in the hospital.

"No, I live on an old farm by the North Sea. Way up in the northernmost part of Denmark." Virginia watched Hannah with a caring look in her eyes that spread to a broad smile when a loud fart came from the bed that even the comforter couldn't muffle.

Hannah's cheeks turned red, and she looked down at her feet. "Sorry. I didn't mean to. I'll hold it back next time."

"Hold back your farts! No, no, don't ever do that. You certainly mustn't, my sweet girl. The wind and the weather must take their course, as I always say. It's only natural to fart; if you hold back a fart, you'll get a tummy ache." Virginia struck a proper sympathy fart and grinned at the sight of Hannah's countenance. "Too many people have a weird old-fashioned taboo about farting and I hate anything that resembles prejudice. Everyone has the right to live their life as they wish without others interfering and telling them it's not appropriate." She removed a hairpin from her bun and scratched her cheek before putting the hairpin back in place, all the while smiling lovingly at Hannah. "I understand you have been involved in an accident."

Hannah nodded reluctantly. She wasn't ready to think about the horrible experience of sitting in a car with a knife to her chest. It was much better to do what she used to and try to suppress her feelings. Nothing good ever came from showing emotions. And she felt an illogical guilt and shame so deep that it had to be buried. It was her fault that not one but two people had died.

Virginia let the question pass and said instead: "All people must follow their journey along the River of Life, and you are well on yours. You are almost grown up, and it has been a rough trip so far, with waterfalls and whirlpools to pass."

Hannah nodded. It made sense to her. She kept dreaming of a river and how to stay afloat without being washed away by the water.

Virginia continued: "I'd love to teach you how to use your common sense to make the journey along the River of Life easier, more enjoyable, and, most importantly, how to avoid going down the wrong tributaries and wasting precious time finding the right way back. But for now, just remember that a young river always is wild and difficult to control. The more mature a river becomes, the smoother the bottom becomes and the wild currents slow down. That's how it will work for you too." She was about to start a new conversation when a doctor came in with a brochure in his hand, and Virginia got up immediately.

"When will I see you again?" Hannah was reluctant to let go of Virginia's hand.

"Tomorrow, my sweet girl. I'll be back tomorrow. First, you must sleep."

It didn't take long for Hannah to fall into a restless sleep and immediately start dreaming. But it was a dream she didn't want to dream—a dream that kept her trapped in what she had been trying to escape. A dream that took her back to her childhood, when her journey down the River of Life began. In her sleep, she squirmed and hid her face, clinging to the pain, for it was the only thing real and constant in her life. It was the only thing that would keep her afloat.

Chapter 1

The river was young and fierce. It flowed fast and uncontrollably, filled with insidious eddies and dangerous areas of rocks and small waterfalls.

For as long as Hannah could remember, she had been much taller than her peers. One of the worst things she knew was when someone she met for the first time assumed she was much older than she was and started talking to her and saying things she didn't understand.

No one ever took the time to get to know her. They just looked at her and assumed she understood what they were saying. And then, when they realized she didn't, they either got annoyed and stopped talking to her, or they started talking as if she was less gifted.

Frustration and embarrassment and shame at not understanding what was being said to her ruled her life from a very young age, and it made her even more withdrawn. But it also made her even more determined to learn and excel. She hated the attention she got when people found out she was so young, and she learned early on to bend her neck and appear smaller than she was.

Hannah often woke up with sweat on her forehead at night and turned on the bedside light. It was that disgusting dream again, the dream about the river. In the river, she couldn't control her journey, where she was taken or where she would end up. The waters just carried her along. It was terrifying, and she wished, as she had so often before, that she had a brother or sister to comfort her and make her feel safe and loved. But the only thing in her lonely life was the pain.

There was the pain of missing—an immense and unquenchable pain. The pain of feeling unwanted—not loved, not appreciated.

Hannah's first experience with that kind of pain was when she was three, desperately trying to get her father's attention.

"Dad," Hannah pulled him by the pant leg. "Daddy, I can read." She held a newspaper almost larger than herself. "It says old houses are..."

"Read? You're just a little girl. Little girls can't read newspapers."

A headline on the front page caught her father's eye. "Let me see that paper." He grabbed it and began to read. Hannah pulled tentatively at his trouser leg again, but he was utterly engrossed in the newspaper.

Hannah hadn't managed to get his attention then, or in the years that followed. She vaguely remembered having her mother's attention when she was a baby, but that was so long ago that it could easily be something she imagined.

Growing up, Hannah had never had a solid anchor point or lifeline thrown out to her. There was no one who loved her, no one who cared for her. Sure, there were the occasional women who came to clean and look after the apartment, but they were just paid helpers and didn't pay attention to the lonely little girl.

Every time Hannah allowed herself to hope that things were different, that she would finally be loved by someone, by anyone, that hope crashed down to the ground like a—like the time she turned ten, and her father actually remembered her birthday, saying, "When you're off school, come to the 'Magazine.' Then we'll go to the warehouse and find you a nice present."

Hannah rushed to the apartment, dropped her school bag, and ran to the building where her father worked, otherwise known as the 'Magazine.' She was going gift shopping with her father! She couldn't imagine anything better!

He wanted to spend time with her! She was thrilled. She thought that she was loved, after all. Hannah excitedly walked into the reception area, where a chic young woman was sorting out letters on a desk.

"Uh..." Hannah stammered. "My ... my father is expecting me."

"Your father?" The woman stared at Hannah with a blank expression on her face.

"Yes, John..." Hannah looked down at the floor shyly, her excitement quickly evaporating.

"Are you my boss's daughter?" The lady looked at her in amazement. "I had no idea he had a daughter!"

Hannah remained silent, as there was no sensible response.

"You're tall." She stared inquisitively at Hannah, as if she had fallen from another planet, before picking up the phone. "Your daughter is here.... Okay, I'll tell her." The receptionist looked at Hannah. "I was told to inform you that he doesn't have time anyway. Your father forgot to include you in his calendar."

Hannah turned and walked away without a word. Her father had forgotten all about her. Sadly, she wasn't that surprised. She was more surprised that she actually had gotten her hopes up in the first place. His job was obviously more important than his only daughter. She was about to burst into tears, but suddenly remembered something she had read recently—*Don't cry over anything that won't cry over you!* She had recently read it in one of the thick books she had borrowed from the library, and it suited her situation perfectly. There was no need to cry when nobody cared. As a result of her parents' indifference and lack of love and care, Hannah became isolated and unable to show emotion. She didn't see the point of expressing herself when there was no one to reassure her or express themselves back. She learned from a young age to keep her feelings to herself and to build walls around her heart to protect it from the emptiness that threatened to engulf her.

Her parents provided for her physically. There was always money in the kitchen drawer, and Hannah could buy whatever she wanted. But all the material goods in the world couldn't compensate for her parents' lack of time, attention, and love.

Hannah couldn't remember exactly when she realized her parents were unlike others. They had absolutely nothing in common and hardly ever spoke to each other. On more than one occasion, Hannah had noticed her mother shutting herself away in the master bedroom with a man, usually someone several years younger than herself. Loud squeals and laughter followed by moans and screams came from inside the bedroom, and Hannah was quite aware of what was happening, even though her mother used to say they were working on a project. Her mother had never worked a single hour in her life, so it didn't quite add up.

Her father slept at the other end of their large apartment and was so rarely home that he probably didn't know what was going on with her mother and her "co-workers." Even if he had known, though, Hannah doubted he would have cared. She had also seen him several times in town, with a pretty lady hanging off his arm. No, her parents had their own lives, and she could do nothing to change it.

One of the few joys Hannah had was the quiet moments when she sat in the red leather chair in the living room—Arne Jacobsen's famous and precious designer chair, called 'The Egg.' There, she could sit quietly for hours, immersing herself in books and newspapers and forgetting her utter loneliness. Words were her whole life.

She loved words and read everything she could get her hands on, storing everything in her sponge of a brain.

Hannah not only found solace in her books, but also in her beloved crayons. She drew and colored the drawings, and cherished each one of them, turning them into her own little works of art. She would leave each finished drawing on the desk in her father's office, hoping that one day he would call her in and tell her how talented she was. That never happened, and she became increasingly introverted over the years. She could never quite understand why no one cared about her.

One morning, when Hannah came out of her room ready to go to school, her father stopped her. "Come here, girl!" He turned his back to her and raised a hand above his head. "You've grown so much. You're taller than me now! And you're only twelve."

Hannah corrected him, "I'm eleven."

But her father once again failed to hear her, disappearing out the door without a second glance. It was a familiar feeling for her, one that had become all too common over the years. With a sigh, she decided to take solace in one of her favorite pastimes, walking. She slipped out the door and went to the stairs. The familiar rhythm of her long legs running down the stairs always seemed to soothe her troubled mind.

Despite living in a grand apartment and attending a prestigious school, Hannah had never been one to be swayed by material possessions. The only advantage she saw in her apartment that most people would have envied was its prime location in the heart of Copenhagen, where she could lose herself in the bustling energy of the city, like she was about to do now. For her, it was the simple pleasures in life that held the most value, like the feeling of the old cobblestone under her bare feet, the sound of the wind rustling through the trees in the park, or the sight of the sun setting over the horizon.

As she walked, she couldn't help but wonder what it would be like to have parents who actually saw her, who cared about her. But deep down, she knew that it was a futile thought. She had learned to rely on herself, to be her own anchor in a world that seemed determined to leave her adrift.

Copenhagen became her ally. She loved the city and the way she could disappear into the crowd. She loved being able to listen and absorb knowledge without actively participating in what was happening around her. She moved quickly and effortlessly through the old cobbled streets on her long legs.

She had a fixed tour that she walked almost every day. The first stop on her route was always the 'Magazine,' the big old building that had been home to the country's largest newspaper since 1916. The building where her father was the top manager, the place that took her father from her day after agonizing day. Standing outside the building on the opposite side, looking up at the windows on the second floor where her father had his big office, she always imagined him opening the window and waving to her, calling her, and asking her to come in. But it never happened, and after standing there waiting for a while, she gave up, and continued down to Nyhavn, where the beautiful old houses painted in rainbow colors stood solidly next to each other. Nyhavn was also where the world-famous Danish author Hans Christian Andersen had lived for many years. The sunny side, the northeast side, was the one that was always busy. Thousands went in and out of the cozy restaurants or visited one of the many taverns.

But Hannah preferred the tranquility on the opposite side of the old canal, excavated by Swedish prisoners of war more than three hundred years ago. On the quiet side of Nyhavn, she could look across the canal at the beautiful buildings and the many people enjoying their lives. Hannah could sit down for hours with her sketchbook, drawing and watching life go on around her.

Her journey home always took her across Kongens Nytorv, where she would stop in front of the great equestrian statue erected in 1688 as a tribute to King Christian V. It was raised because the people loved their king so much. Every time she saw that statue, she felt a strange kind of envy mixed with the hope that one day there would be people who loved her so much that they would give her something unique. Hannah sighed and sprinted through Strøget and up to Storkespringvandet, the beautiful old fountain with the three giant storks.

The storks had long legs like her, but it was the frogs Hannah liked to watch most. To her, the frogs symbolized change, the change from egg to tadpole to frog—a change she was waiting for herself. Hannah's secret hope was that she was still just an egg and one day, she would go through the process of changing to become something else—into what, she wasn't sure, but something she would be proud to be.

Hannah always walked three times around the fountain before walking on with quick steps up through the old street that led to her favorite place, Rundetårn. There, she would marvel at the magnificent old observatory—the beautiful tower built by King Christian X and completed in 1642.

Several times a week, she walked up the two hundred meters of ancient stone along the exciting, snaking path that twisted seven and a half times around the tower's core before flattening out on the viewing platform.

High above the bustle of the city, thirty-five meters above street level, Hannah felt like a perfectly normal girl, not someone who was too tall, too thin, and insecure. It was a lovely feeling, and she tried to hold onto it for as long as possible.

Most days, she went straight home from there, but once a week, she made a detour to the main library, where thousands of books stood side by side, waiting for her to devour them.

When she picked certain books, such as about philosophy or Italian cooking, the elderly librarian would look her up and down and ask, "Aren't you too young to read that sort of thing?"

"I like to cook." Hannah accidentally let out a loud fart, and several faces turned to her.

The librarian blinked at her and pointed to a corner of the large room. "The restroom is right over there..."

Hannah sighed and walked back into the street. It was so weird that she farted so much. It wasn't like she was going to the toilet. It was just air that was in her. She had observed that other people were able to fart almost silently, and she wished she knew how they did it. She sighed again and started walking back towards the big lonely apartment. As always, she couldn't wait but opened one of the books and started reading as she walked. She walked slower and slower and her eyes slid over the densely written pages with fascination.

The words in the books couldn't hurt her. She could cry over a story, but then it would be out of pity for others, not pity for herself. The words couldn't bully, tease, and make her cry, like the other students did in school.

Hannah hated school. The other students teased and bullied her all day long. She had no close friends—she was too tall, too unique, and too bright. They were jealous (or so the teachers would tell her) and found a thousand ways to tease her. Her low status began on the first day of first grade, and nothing could make it different. The reason for this she did not understand, even though she was very aware that she was different from the others. She was half a head taller than the tallest of her classmates, and her trousers and blouses were always too short. And, of course, it was impossible to wear a dress because it barely covered her bottom.

But why there wasn't a single boy or girl in the class who liked her, she couldn't understand. Was her height really that big a problem, or was something else wrong with her? Hannah came to hate mirrors, and she learned to avoid looking at herself in the years to come. She had no idea, therefore, that she was developing into a rare beauty—a beauty that came from within—a beauty enhanced by her beautiful brown hair that always curled around her face and shone in myriad browns and golds.

She was extremely bright and quick-thinking. But she had learned to keep a strictly low profile from that first day of the first grade. So, hardly any of her teachers knew exactly how bright and capable she was.

The first day in sixth grade, Hannah tried to sneak into the classroom unseen, but she was nearly impossible to overlook. Her biggest tormentor came up behind her and kicked her in the back of the knee.

"Ouch, damn it!" Hannah slumped, trying to keep her balance.

"Now you look almost normal in size." Lars grinned wickedly and kicked her again, this time across the groin. Lars was half a head shorter than her, small, tight, and broad across the shoulders. "Knitting needle," he shouted, laughing again.

Hannah turned red, and tears welled up in her eyes. Not for one second did she think she could fight back or retaliate. She never told anyone about her feelings. She just took everything in and somehow blamed herself, as if everything she was going through was her own fault. If someone had asked her why it was her fault, she wouldn't have been able to give a sensible answer. There was no reasonable answer to her guilty feelings.

But she had learned the art of disappearing into herself. When things got more than she could handle, she could faint inside and envelop herself into a soothing gray fog. This skill would prove important, and one she came to use many times before she learned to navigate the River of Life.

Chapter 2

A small sandbar appeared in the turbulent river and created a respite, a well-deserved break on which to relax and recuperate after the trip through the raging current.

From the hallway, Hannah watched the math teacher checking out his new students. Twenty-eight girls and boys, aged twelve to fourteen, lined the walls. Several of the girls were on the verge of becoming women. Hannah looked at their blank faces with astonishment. Some of them had started wearing makeup during the summer vacation and looked much older than their age.

Hannah sighed deeply before she walked into the classroom with her head bowed, not watching where she was going. She had deliberately stalled to ensure all her classmates had arrived.

"Ouch." The math teacher frowned, as Hannah tried to hurry past him, but instead bumped into him.

Hannah mentally prepared herself for one of those silly remarks about her height—she was used to those. In her mind, she was already trying to figure out which of the overused phrases he was preparing to say. But he didn't say any of them.

The teacher placed his hand on her shoulder. "Impressive!" He observed her thoughtfully. There was no hint of makeup on her face and no jewelry or adornments. "Stand over here." He led her to the wall and gently nudged her into a vacant spot between two boys, both a head shorter than her.

The math teacher went back to the desk and grabbed his briefcase.

"Skyscraper," Lars whispered, sticking his tongue out, pulling Hannah's hair, and making her cringe. She felt tears welling up in her eyes, but she refused to give Lars the satisfaction of seeing her cry. Suddenly she noticed that the teacher was looking at her intently. She wondered if he was going to scold her, but to her surprise, he seemed more interested in her than angry.

Hannah could feel that there was something special about her that fascinated the teacher. She tried to concentrate on the lesson, but it was difficult when she was sitting in the front row by the window, right next to where the teacher was standing.

The teacher kept looking at her and more than once he seemed to lose concentration. Hannah saw him getting more and more annoyed and she had a strange feeling that she was the cause even though she didn't understand what she had done. She had no idea that it was because he felt completely enchanted by her intelligent eyes.

While the teacher wrote an equation on the blackboard, Hannah tried to solve it in her head. She knew the answer, but she was afraid to raise her hand. It wouldn't do any good to draw attention to herself again. Who knew what Lars would think of to tease her next? The math teacher looked at his students and said, "Let me see some fingers. Who has the answer to that equation? It's from last year's syllabus, and you should be able to solve it easily."

No one raised a finger.

He frowned irritably. "Haven't you learned anything at all?" He pointed to a little guy with glasses sitting in the front row. "Up to the board. You must be able to solve it..."

The boy sighed and stood up. "It's too difficult. We haven't learned much about equations yet."

The teacher waved the boy back down. "So, there's no one? Not one of you who can solve the simple equation?"

"Fifty-six." Hannah looked down at the table. She wished she could shrink into a mouse hole. She should have kept her mouth shut, but the answer had just slipped out.

"Can you explain how you got that result? Please come up to the board and show the others how to do it. Show me."

Hannah sighed and stood up to her full height. She was already over six feet tall at the age of twelve.

As if in a trance, Hannah took the chalk the teacher handed her and stood motionless for a minute before hurriedly writing the necessary figures and putting two lines under the result. Then she slowly turned to the teacher.

"You're very bright," he nodded appreciatively. "Can you solve this one too?" He took the chalk from her and quickly wrote a long equation under her calculations. He handed the chalk back to her. "Just take your time," he said.

Hannah frowned and considered for a short moment before she began to write with a confident hand, finishing by putting the obligatory two lines under the result.

The teacher waved her down into place.

Hannah had a strange feeling that he could see right through her. That he knew something about her that the other teachers couldn't see. It almost seemed as if he couldn't take his eyes off her. As if he thought she was special. But that couldn't be true, could it? She was just that tall girl who was easy to tease. She sighed. All she wanted was to fit in and be like the others, but she knew that was impossible.

For the next few months, math class was Hannah's great joy. She got to experience acceptance and appreciation for nearly the first time. Her teacher never allowed the other children to bully her. But for all the good that math provided, recess was the opposite—the worst time of the day. Lars became more and more inventive in his teasing. He was hounding her constantly.

"Giraffe girl, go back to the zoo where you belong," Lars said, as he tried to poke her in the chest, hitting her stomach instead and causing her to crumple with a gasp. She wasn't mature enough to understand that this was his first attempt to make erotic contact. She just wished he would leave her alone.

After recess there was math, but for once Hannah was silent and sat with her head bowed, sniffling and not listening. Why the teasing today hit her so hard, she did not know. But she felt more depressed and unhappy than usual.

When the bell rang and the other children hurried out, the teacher came down to her.

Is something wrong? It's not like you to be so quiet.

Hannah didn't answer but started crying loudly and the math teacher reached out his hand and pulled her to her feet.

He looked up at her tearful face and Hannah couldn't help but see that there was genuine compassion in his eyes. Compassion, but also something else she didn't understand. He looked at her a bit like the hero in the books she sometimes borrowed from the library. He looked at her as if she were a grown woman. And not just any woman, but a woman he liked. Hannah sniffled and didn't dare to look at him. "It's okay ... I'll leave now." Her big brown eyes were filled with tears, and she had an expression of hopelessness all around her.

"Did they tease you again?"

She nodded, and the teacher's kind voice made her break down completely. She sobbed as if her heart was going to break. "They all hate me. Why was I born? Answer me?" She looked reproachfully at her teacher. "Why was I born when neither my mother nor father care about me? There's nothing but pain and hopelessness in sight, and I can't bear it any longer."

Something about her appearance made her seem very mature for her age. It shone through clearly even though she was crying and miserable. The teacher stepped right up to her and gently touched her arm. "Come, let me comfort you."

At that moment, he seemed to forget he was her teacher. He seemed to forget that she was only twelve and they were standing in the middle of a classroom, where everyone outside the courtyard and walking by in the hallway could see them. He seemed to forget everything but the beautiful, young, unhappy girl he was hugging.

Hannah's violent sobbing stopped, and she sniffled. She was conscious that something was happening but did not quite understand it.

"Little girl," he murmured, bending her head down to level it with his mouth. "Little, darling girl, don't be sad. The other kids are being silly, and I'll make sure they stop bullying and teasing you."

Hannah pressed her young breasts against his body, enjoying the feeling of his arms around her. It was the first time she could remember someone giving her a proper hug—the first time she experienced a feeling that everything was going to be okay.

"Dear beautiful girl. You don't know how special you are." The teacher pressed a gentle kiss to her lips.

They forgot time and place and stood close together, enjoying perfect harmony.

"What the hell is going on here?" The principal's angry voice interrupted the séance. Embarrassed, Hannah quickly grabbed her school bag and ran out the door, head bowed, leaving it to her math teacher to explain what had happened.

She was already aware that things would never be the same again, and that it was her fault. Everything was her fault. She was already dreading the next day's math class. And her fears proved well-founded.

A little pointy-nosed woman stood up in front of the class. "You'll have me in math for the rest of the year. I'm afraid there are some, and I won't mention any names." But she looked stiffly at Hannah as she spoke and repeated, "Unfortunately, some people don't know how to behave when they're almost grown up and should know better."

Chapter 3

Out of the rushing waters of the river, a small island appeared. An island just big enough for two. The little island was a lovely haven, but it was only a short time before the river came rushing, flooded, and swallowed the island, leaving no trace.

Sixth grade had been her worst year so far and she missed her old math teacher. She had never heard a single word from him, but she hoped he had found another school with nice students. Hannah picked up her school bag. Finally, it was the weekend, and it had been a rough week. Lars and the others had teased her even more than usual, but thankfully, the school year was almost over. Maybe things would change when she started seventh grade after the summer break. Hannah bowed her head and walked out into the schoolyard.

A short, dark-haired guy suddenly appeared before her with a big smile on his tanned face. "Those long legs look cool!" he exclaimed.

Hannah looked startled and tried to duck. At twelve years old, she was already much taller than everyone else, and there was no sign that she would stop growing. She had grown a quarter of a foot just in the last month.

"My name is Henry, and I'm going to school here. I'm just visiting today, but I'll start in earnest on Monday."

Hannah looked down at him with her eyes wide open and felt a strange warm feeling inside. She suddenly began to stutter. "My name is Ha-Ha-Hannah. I'm in the sixth grade. B. Jensen's class."

"I'm told that's the school where the Danish Queen went. Do you know if it's true?"

Hannah nodded.

"My mother told me it's one of the most prestigious schools in Copenhagen."

Hannah nodded again, and then let out a silent fart, feeling utter joy. Finally! There was a boy who wanted to talk to her! And he really wanted to talk to her, not just teasing.

"Would you like a piece of chocolate?" Henry rummaged in his school bag and pulled out half a slab of milk chocolate.

Hannah's eyes sparkled. "I love chocolate! Thank you!"

"It's the same color as your eyes," Henry said, looking up at her golden-brown eyes, entranced. "Chocolate eyes..."

Hannah chuckled and broke off a piece of chocolate. "You have a funny accent."

"I'm not so used to speaking Danish. I'm from America."

"Are you going to live here in Copenhagen?"

Henry shrugged. "I don't know."

"Are you here with your parents?"

"Only my mother." Henry looked away and muttered, "Do your parents fight too?"

"No, they're never home." Hannah would have liked to ask more about his parents, but she could tell he didn't want to talk about himself.

There was something strange about that boy. It was as if they had met before. They smiled at each other, and it felt like they were the only people in the schoolyard.

"What's your favorite subject?" Henry grabbed her hand and led her to a bench in the far corner of the yard. No one had ever done that before.

Hannah was about to answer when she saw her biggest tease, Lars, rushing toward them.

"Be careful. He's strong." Hannah let go of Henry's hand and tried to get in front of the much smaller Henry to protect him. Henry quickly pushed her away and stood directly before Lars.

The two boys of the same age had little in common.

Lars was already taking shape as a man. His shoulders were getting firm, and strong muscles were developing under the fat. His blond hair and blue eyes highlighted his prominent jawline, and his hands and feet were large and powerful. It was obvious he was in the habit of using them.

On the other hand, Henry was slim and slender, with thin wrists and ankles, much like a girl. His hair was an indeterminate brown color that spiked down over his neck. The prettiest thing about him was his warm brown eyes, filled with a calm intelligence.

"Who the fuck are you? A small piece of shit?" Lars nudged Henry. "You aren't too damn smart to be with her, the Monster girl from another planet." Henry didn't answer but made a few quick movements with his hands and body, and before Hannah could blink her eyes, to her astonishment, she saw Lars flop backward and land on his back in the middle of a puddle.

Henry didn't dignify Lars with a glance but brushed some imaginary dust off his shoe with the leg of his pants. "Are you coming?" He held out his hand to Hannah.

"What did you do?" Hannah was flabbergasted. He had saved her. Saved her from being teased. No one had ever done that before either.

"It was just a simple karate move." Henry dismissed it and looked up at her admiring gaze. "Where can we be alone?"

Hannah led him out through the school's green gate, where they found themselves in a large cobbled square.

"Is..ra..el..s Plads..." Henry carefully spelled the street name on the house's wall. "What does it mean?"

"It's something about the Jews and the city of Israel. Something to do with the twenty-fifth anniversary of the rescue of the Danish Jews during World War II." Hannah pulled him by the sleeve. "Come on; we're going to the park. There are a lot of huge rhododendrons. Giant bushes you can crawl under if you want to hide." She definitely knew all the good hiding places. Hannah led Henry over the topped cobbles, across the old square, and through the wrought iron gate into the pleasant old park.

Henry didn't relinquish her hand for a second, and Hannah was in seventh heaven. A large statue on the shore of a lake caught Henry's eye.

"Who's that?"

"H. C. Ørsted. He invented electromagnetism."

"You really know a lot." Henry looked at her admiringly.

Hannah suddenly felt happy and proud that she knew so much about her city. All her many trips around the city had not been in vain.

"Have you had lunch?" Henry asked. "If not, we could buy some food and eat here."

"I never eat lunch; I've reached my weight limit," Hannah said, suddenly feeling stupid.

"That's silly. You have to eat something," he said.

"If I don't eat so much, I'll probably stop growing."

"Why would you stop growing?" Henry looked up at her. "You're stunningly beautiful as you are; if you get any taller, you'll get even more beautiful. You don't have to be like everyone else; you have to be unique. You are one of those people others look up to."

Hannah giggled. "Yes, look up to me; they already do."

"Yeah, but not just because you're tall and pretty. Everybody must also look up to you because you're sweet, kind, helpful, and talented. But that's who you are, and I know you'll be even more so as you get older and more experienced."

Hannah had tears in her eyes. "That's the most beautiful thing anyone has ever said to me."

"You ARE beautiful," Henry said quietly and confidently. Hannah lit up and looked down at Henry with a smile in her eyes.

"Am I?" she asked, gasping.

"Without a doubt," he said, looking up at her.

"I don't believe you."

"It doesn't matter whether you believe me or not. The fact is that I think you're beautiful."

Hannah blushed, and her ears buzzed. She was afraid tears would well up in her eyes. She could tell Henry meant what he said. Something was appreciating in his voice, and his brown eyes had an intelligent and honest look.

Henry continued, watching her through the foliage of the rhododendron bush. "This might be something you'll struggle with for a while. People might act weird around you 'cause you're tall, good-looking, and smart. Some dudes might even be scared of you 'cause of all that! But don't worry, it's not your fault. You just gotta be patient with them and keep being yourself."

"What nonsense." Hannah was about to fart and didn't dare look at Henry, but he didn't comment on it and didn't seem to feel bothered by a bit of hot air.

Henry took her hand. "It's not nonsense. You wait and see in the years to come; you're going to be rich and famous. But first, you need to learn something important about yourself. Can I kiss you?" He jumped into the subject and looked at her hopefully.

"Uh, yeah." Hannah suddenly didn't feel too tall and weird and different.

She was a girl that a boy admired. At once, she felt like the others in the school who always bragged about their boyfriends.

Hannah didn't hesitate; she wrapped her arms around him and pressed her lips against his cheek.

Henry wriggled free. "That's not what I meant." His honest eyes looked up into hers. "Bend down a little so I can reach you, and stand still."

Hannah obeyed, her eyes lighting up and her mouth opening.

Henry planted a gentle kiss on her open lips. "You're the most beautiful girl I've ever seen, that's for sure. Thank you so much for the kiss."

"You're welcome." Hannah was perplexed. His lips had felt very different than she had imagined. They weren't as soft as she'd expected. They were hard and felt strong. Strong in a weird way. They made her lips tingle and yearn for more.

"You won't let the other boys do the same, promise?" Henry asked. Hannah nodded, unable to find her words. She felt empty-headed.

"I'd like to kiss you again some other time if that's okay with you?" Henry looked at her adoringly. "You're the most beautiful girl in the whole world."

A tear rolled down Hannah's cheek, and Henry wiped it away with his thumb.

"Can I kiss you again some other time?"

"Yes," Hannah nodded energetically. "Yes, you may. I liked it; it was lovely."

"Will you promise me you'll never kiss Lars?" Henry was serious as they stood outside Hannah's doorway, unwilling to say goodbye.

Hannah nodded, unable to say anything.

"I'll see you on Monday." Henry waved at her and disappeared around the corner towards the station.

Hannah would always remember the disappointment of coming to school on Monday and spending the whole day looking for him. Every day for weeks, the first thing she did when she got to school was look for a little dark-haired boy who had given her the best day of her life.

"Oh dear, that little scab won't be back; you've scared him away, Monster girl," Lars grinned evilly.

Chapter 4

The little sandbank that once provided rest was flooded by the raging river, which continued its wild course and suddenly changed shape. It narrowed and ran through a steep gorge, surrounded by high mountains that engulfed the river and made it impossible to see where it was leading.

For the next three years, Hannah evolved from child to teenager. She dreamt of the raging river almost every night and felt as if she was drowning.

"Mom!" Hannah gently opened her mother's bedroom door. "Are you alone?" It was obvious that she wasn't, because Hannah managed to see a dark head before it disappeared under the covers.

"What is it now? Can't you see I'm working."

"I'm bleeding."

"Oh, it's only natural. Why are you bothering me with that? There are sanitary towels in the bathroom cabinet. You take the ones you need. There are pills in the medicine cabinet too if you are in pain. It's nothing dangerous. Just your period; you must know that, right?" Her mother chirped to a bare hairy male leg emerging from the duvet.

Hastily, Hannah withdrew from the door, wondering if she was the only one with such crazy parents. She couldn't help but wonder if there was something inherently wrong with her, something that made her different from other kids her age, so that her parents could not love her. In a strange subconscious way, she felt that it was her fault that they were behaving so strangely. Her parents behaved completely different from the parents she read about in the many books in which she loved to immerse herself. They all seemed so loving and like they actually cared a great deal about their children.

Trying to push those thoughts aside, she took a deep breath and focused on the task at hand. Opening the closet, she rifled through the shelves until she found what she was looking for—a packet of sanitary towels. With some difficulty, she placed one in her panties. While this was all new, she could clearly feel the physical changes happening within her body.

Her breasts, which had previously been quite small, had grown significantly in the last few months. She hesitantly touched her left breast and felt the pink nipple grow and stiffen. Startled, she released her grip. But the feeling of her fingers stayed with her long after and she tried to suppress them, curling up in the leather chair with the thickest book she could find. She wasn't at all sure she wanted to grow up and take responsibility. The fact that she was already doing that didn't even cross her mind.

Hannah still loved her walks around old Copenhagen, and over the years, her observant eyes discovered that there were many different types of people. Some were open and trusting, and they seemed thoroughly happy and content, walking around with smiles, spreading positivity wherever they went. Hannah soon understood that a positive attitude toward life had nothing to do with whether you had expensive clothes and nice shoes or you were one of the homeless beggars sitting at the train station. It was something that came from within.

On one of her many walks through Copenhagen's cobblestone streets, she came across a shop she hadn't seen before. Curious, she went to the window and looked at the display. Leather clothes with zips and chains were everywhere, and boots with heels so high, she thought it must have been impossible to walk in them. Hannah stepped closer. There was something about those boots that spoke to her in a way she had never experienced before. It was as if they were trying to tell her something.

"Hello, tall girl. You're welcome to come in and try them on!" An older gray-haired man with a ponytail and tattoos all over his arms looked at her admiringly. "You'll look stunning in a pair of stilettos like that. How about those long boots there?" He nodded towards the boots that she had been examining.

Hannah shook her head. "No, I only wear flats. I'm so tall..." At fifteen, she measured over six feet tall barefoot.

"That's silly; you'd look excessively hot." The man let his gaze slide up and down her until it stopped at her breasts, young and bouncing against her tight blouse.

Hannah walked further down Strøget and looked at the windows. There were so many fancy clothes, but she knew none would fit her. Still, a pair of washed jeans with rivets attracted her like a magnet. She had to try them on.

"How did they fit?" The helpful saleswoman stood outside the fitting room, waiting. Hannah handed her the pants without saying anything.

"Poor girl, it must be tough being so tall," the other assistant whispered, winking at her colleague.

Hannah looked at the women with resignation and disappeared from the shop. Damn it, those pants had looked long on the mannequin, but when she put them on, they were at least four inches too short.

Summer had come suddenly the year she was fifteen, and it was swelteringly hot and damp even though it was ten at night. There always seemed to be shouting, laughter, and music coming from the street from lots of young people having fun. Most days, Hannah was satisfied sitting in the egg chair reading or standing at her easel painting. But there were other days when she would sit alone in her room in the big apartment and stare at the wall—days when Hannah dreamed of having a friend. She wished for another girl with whom she could share her innermost thoughts and feelings—a girl who wanted to be friends with her.

There were also days when she dreamed her first vague dreams of love and that glorious day when it would come to her. One of those days, when her thoughts were extra strong about love and someone for whom to care, she decided to do something she had never done before. Usually, she stayed in the apartment when it was dark outside, but today she felt something different was about to happen. She grabbed her keys, put on a pair of flat shoes, and quickly ran down the stairs and into the street, directly into the pulsating nightlife.

At first, she stayed close to the walls, taking care not to be in the glow of the streetlamps. But slowly, she became attracted to all the excitement of the street and suddenly found herself directly under the light of one of the big old streetlamps.

Several young people pushed her and laughed at her because she was so tall.

"Fuck, you're huge."

"What did your mother give you to eat?"

"Long legs and nice tits." One of the guys looked at her slim body, with the young, firm breasts.

Hannah retreated to the safety of the darkness along the wall and had almost decided to go back home when she spotted him.

The man of her dreams—a tall man. He was leaning against the gate that led into the cemetery. His blond hair was long, and he stood with a lit cigarette in his hand. At his feet stood a half-filled bottle of some type of clear liquid. The man caught Hannah's eye and extinguished the cigarette by flicking off the glow. He bent down and took a big swig from the bottle before lazily walking towards her.

He handed the bottle to her. "Hey, tall girl, you need a sip? It's top-quality vodka."

Hannah reached out as if in a trance and took a good swig from the bottle. The strong liquor stung her throat, and she began to cough. She had never tasted alcohol before.

The guy grinned. "I guess you're not used to that. Come on." He took a firm grip on her elbow and led her into the cemetery right next to the noisy pedestrian street. "I'm Anders, and now you and I will have some fun."

"Fun? What's happening there?" Hannah didn't understand why he wanted to enter the cemetery. It was dark and quiet and pretty creepy.

Anders grinned but didn't answer. "Are you a virgin?"

Hannah nodded timidly, hoping he wouldn't walk away.

"That's great; then you get to experience the pain. Without pain, there is no pleasure. But you're going to have to wait a bit. After all, when you're a virgin, you're not protected."

"Protected? What do you mean?"

"You can get fucking pregnant, and I don't want any fucking babies, so we'll get you on the pill first. But you can do me a favor."

"Favor?" Hannah was intrigued and more than willing. Someone needing something from her was entirely new to her. "What do you want me to do?"

Anders released her arm. "Are you ready to see how big I am?"

Hannah nodded enthusiastically but didn't say anything. She wanted to see what a man had between his legs. Maybe even touch it. Those thoughts were starting to come to her more and more often lately. She had been looking in the brightly colored magazines her father kept in his study. There were naked men and women in the photos. While it hadn't stirred a single emotion in her, Hannah knew there must be something different and more exciting in the relationship between a man and a woman.

"Then lie down here." Anders nudged her to the ground without regard for where she landed.

The sharp, cold tombstone drilling into her back made her moan in pain. The tall man took no notice but unzipped his pants, pulled out his stiff cock and sat on top of her.

Hannah gasped. It certainly didn't look like the ones she'd seen on the sculptures in the park, and she also had a hard time seeing the similarity between the stiff throbbing cock he held out to her and the pictures she'd seen in her father's magazines.

"You're so big. That's going to hurt."

"Yes, I'm big." Anders laughed. "And without pain, there is no pleasure. Always remember that. Pain always comes with pleasure. But like I said before, you'll have to wait a while before you get it. I'm not having a fucking baby, and the condoms you can buy are too fucking small, so you'll have to take the pill." He thrust his stiff cock towards her. "Touch it," he commanded. Automatically and without thinking, she took it in her hand and started rubbing it.

"It's getting all wet," Hannah's eyes widened as liquid came out of the tip.

"Keep at it; it needs a woman's hand."

Suddenly he let out a roar that made her cringe in fright and let go of him.

"Don't stop; I'm about to cum." He grabbed her hard by the neck and held her tight. "Rub, for fuck's sake."

A hot sticky splash landed on her face and ran down between her breasts.

"You're my girl now." Anders zipped his pants and pulled Hannah to her feet. "I'll take care of you."

Hannah wiped her face with her hand and met his gaze. "Do you want to take care of me?"

He grinned, "Well, of course. Why do you think I took you in here and gave you a taste of the joys that await you as my girlfriend? It's because I fucking want you."

All her life, no one had ever really wanted her. Hannah sniffled and wiped her eyes. "Okay, if you really mean you will take care of me, then I want to be your girlfriend." She looked admiringly at Anders' swelling upper arms and sighed in deep pleasure. Now she finally had someone who would love her—a knight who would look after her and remove all the obstacles she had in her life.

A sudden thought occurred to her. "But you don't even know my name."

"It doesn't fucking matter," Anders laughed. And Hannah relaxed. It would be nice to have someone take care of her. She looked at him, trying to see what he was thinking. But there was something strange about his eyes. Something that seemed a little scary, almost like he had something to hide.

"I wonder what my parents will say when I tell them I've got a boyfriend." Hannah looked a little concerned. "I have only just turned fifteen."

"Just leave it to me; I'll fix it." Anders grinned and took a firm hold of her arm.

Chapter 5

The narrow gorge squeezed the river, and the water rushed forward at an impossible pace. There was obviously a waterfall ahead. But a vortex in the middle of the river held everything in an iron grip until it suited it to let go and let the rushing current take over again.

Hannah had hardly slept at night fearing that Anders would not come and pick her up as they had agreed. But that fear turned out to be unfounded because he came right after work.

"I love your daughter even though I only met her last night. It was love at first sight. Anyone can see that she is one of a kind." Anders smiled cheekily at Hannah's mother and continued, "I'll take good care of your lovely daughter."

Hannah was beaming with happiness. It was wonderful finally to have someone who loved her and wanted to make decisions for her.

"That's quite a handsome fellow you've found." Hannah's mother let her eyes slide admiringly up and down the young man, and Anders grinned as Hannah's mother reached out and touched his muscular upper arm. "You look so young yourself, it's hard to believe you're old enough to be Hannah's mother." Anders winked mischievously at her and continued, "And your name, Luna, suits you perfectly. It's as beautiful as you."

Hannah watched in silence as jealousy reared its ugly head. Anders was HER boyfriend. Not anyone else's, and certainly not her mother's. Her hopeless mother shouldn't ruin everything by hitting on Anders. Hannah took a firm grip on him. "Anders wants me to move in with him in his apartment. I can do that, can't I? After all, neither you nor Dad are home much, so I'd be better off with Anders."

"Then she can concentrate on her drawings and painting, and if she takes a sabbatical now that she has just finished ninth grade and concentrates on her art, I bet she can get into art school and study." Anders gave Hannah a gentle kiss. "I make a good living as a carpenter, and I can easily support her for a year."

Her mother didn't ask a single question and didn't seem to find it strange that her fifteen-year-old daughter wanted to leave home with a man she had met the night before.

Somewhere deep in her heart, Hannah had hoped that her mother would show some emotion and tell her that she would miss her. But all her mother did was make a pass at Anders.

"Are you going to tell Dad where I am?"

"Yes, yes, of course. Why don't you go inside and pack your things, and I'll entertain Anders for a while..."

It had been no problem for Hannah to be allowed to move, and that very evening, she had picked up all her belongings and moved them all over to Anders' apartment.

"Where do you want me to put my things?" Hannah opened one of the two large suitcases she had brought.

"Here!" Anders kicked at the bottom drawer of an old dresser.

With difficulty, Hannah bent her long body down far enough to open the drawer. "It's already half full..."

"Yes, some of my old clothes I don't wear anymore."

"Can't I take your old clothes out and use the whole drawer for my things?"

"You keep your hands off my clothes. You'll have to make do with half the drawer. We'll put all your other crap we don't have room for here up in the attic. Then you can bring it down when you need it."

Hannah sighed and filled up the drawer with the most necessary of her things. "There isn't much room for two people here."

"Shut the fuck up. There's plenty of room here. It's not like I'm a fucking millionaire."

Hannah looked at the small apartment. A living room doubled as a bedroom, a kitchen, and a tiny bathroom. She had considerably more space in her room at home with her parents, but she tried to convince herself that she was looking forward to her new life with her adult boyfriend.

―

The first night she moved in, Hannah sat at the small dining table, completely absorbed in drawing a portrait of her new adult boyfriend. But it puzzled her and wouldn't come out right. Every time she started drawing Anders' eyes, something went wrong.

"From now on, I'm giving you orders." Anders came in from the bathroom wearing only tight boxers that didn't hide his erection.

Hannah didn't react because she didn't understand what he meant.

"Can't you listen, you bitch? Are you deaf or something?" Anders quickly approached her, sticking his long stiff tongue deep into her right ear.

Hannah screamed in fright and pain. "Don't do that, it hurts. And why are you going to order me around? I don't think that's a good idea."

"I'm the one with the ideas, so naturally, I give orders. Tomorrow we go to the doctor and get birth control pills. Unfortunately, it takes a few weeks for the birth control pills to kick in, so until then, you'll have to give me blowjobs." Anders lifted her with a snap and threw her down on the floor in front of the worn sofa. "Get on your knees and turn your face towards me." He sat down on the sofa and took her face between both hands. Hannah tried to move her head, but he held her down and laid his heavy body over hers. With his teeth, he twisted her blouse open, leaving her proud young breast exposed.

Anders sank his teeth into her nipple and bit down before thrusting his cock into her mouth.

Pain coursed through her, and she presented a huge fart and looked down in shame.

Anders promptly removed his cock from her mouth and slapped her face. "Damn, you stink! You can't lay on my couch and shit like that. You have to hold back," he said harshly. "And by the way, you're getting fat; you must do something about that. I can't show my face in town with a fat girlfriend."

Hannah looked down her slim body in wonder. What did he mean?

Anders switched in one of his sudden mood shifts. "Tell me how much you love me. I need to hear that I'm the only one you love."

Hannah felt the words stuck in her throat. She loved him. Of course she did. But it was difficult to say right after he scolded her.

"Can't you even tell your boyfriend that you love him? You're a shitty girlfriend. Even though I love you, don't be too sure. I wouldn't mind replacing you with someone more willing to fulfill my normal desires."

"You know I love you," Hannah sniffled, looking at Anders with a pleading look in her eyes, and when a dawning understanding hit her, she gently unzipped his pants, knowing what it would take to satisfy him.

He nodded. "That's good. I can see you are beginning to know what I want from you."

Hannah opened her mouth and did her job, and right afterwards Anders disappeared out the door and left Hannah sitting on the floor, confused and unhappy. Where had he gone? Would he come back? Would he still be her boyfriend or would he send her home? She stood up very slowly, engrossed in thoughts. She had to do something. The prospect of going back home, kicked out and unwanted, was unbearable.

~

Later that evening Hannah sat on the toilet for a long time, watching the toilet roll hanging on the wall. The paper cast strange shadows, and in her overheated state of mind, the toilet roll became a guillotine ready to decapitate her. She let out a whimper from deep in her throat and rose slowly. Hesitantly, she stuck a finger in her mouth.

Further in. Further down. Hannah knew she had to do it. With a swift movement, she stuffed her finger down her throat, biting the back of her hand. Hannah began to emit gurgling sounds, and suddenly felt warm vomit all over her hand. She dropped to her knees and stuck her head as far into the toilet bowl as she could. She stayed like that until the last convulsions from her induced vomiting had ceased.

Slowly she got up and flushed the toilet. And along with the water flow, she felt some discomfort being washed away.

She grabbed a bottle of toilet cleaner and quickly cleaned the toilet again. She didn't want Anders to find any trace of her.

She got used to throwing up every morning after Anders left for work and again after lunch and just before he came home from work. Anders never suspected that she was throwing up. Hannah wasn't sure what he would say to that, but she felt strangely guilty and ashamed, and since she could never predict how Anders would react in a given situation, it was safest to keep it to herself. She wanted to make her adult life work. She didn't want to go home again. She had to throw up and hopefully lose some weight so Anders wouldn't think she was getting fat. Not even to herself did she dare to finish the thought that it had been a huge mistake to move in with a man she had just met.

Anders meticulously monitored the calendar as Hannah began taking birth control pills the day after moving in with him, midway through her cycle. It would take seven days for the pills to become effective and provide protection.

Hannah held mixed feelings as the designated time approached. On one hand, she eagerly anticipated it as she was tired of performing oral sex several times a day. Her jaw had also started to hurt. On the other hand, she feared the day she was ready to do it because of Anders' large size, convinced that it would be painful.

The day arrived. And no sooner did Anders get home from work, he stripped off his clothes and lay down on the couch. Immediately, he started rubbing his penis. When it was at its full size, he grabbed Hannah and ripped off her panties. He told her, "Now it's time for you to really feel the pain! Get on top of me and give me a good ride."

"But I'm not ready..." Hannah hesitated, as her fear began to outweigh her curiosity.

"Not ready?" Anders punched her in the stomach. "Nonsense, just get on with it. I've been waiting all day, and now it's time."

Hannah sighed deeply and wrapped her long legs around Anders' stomach and gently sank down against him. When she felt the warm, moist tip begin to enter her, she paused and looked at him, startled.

"You're too big. You're going to tear me apart inside…"

"Shut the fuck up." Anders grabbed her around the waist and forced her down on top of him.

Hannah screamed and tried to jump off, but Anders held on to her tightly and began thrusting harder and harder into her.

Hannah screamed again and began crying. Anders didn't care. He ejaculated, filling her battered body with his juices.

"It was damn good. We'll do it again very soon." Anders turned over on his stomach. "Now I want to sleep. Wake me up when dinner is ready."

On wobbly legs and with tears streaming down her face, Hannah disappeared into the bathroom in confusion. She turned on the hot water in the shower. There was blood on her thighs, and she felt completely shattered and devastated inside and out.

Was that really all there was to it? How could women enjoy sex? She sighed deeply and gently washed her vagina. Well, at least she wasn't a virgin anymore and maybe it was only the first time it hurt so much. Deep down she knew that sex shouldn't feel so painful. But Anders said he loved her, and you were not supposed to hurt the one you loved. She sighed again, got dressed, and started preparing for dinner.

~

After a few months, everything had become routine. In the morning when they woke up, Anders was gentle and loving and told her how much he loved her, and when they had sex, he tried to be gentle so it didn't hurt too much. But when he came home from work he was a completely different person. He had obviously been drinking.

Hannah had already gotten used to Anders drinking a lot and this night was no exception.

Anders took the bottle with him as he staggered to the table. "The chicken is half raw! How hard can it be to fry a chicken? Are you trying to kill me, you fucking bitch?" He poured vodka into his water glass and drained it in one gulp. The only sound during the meal was his steady berating of Hannah and the sound of vodka being poured into a glass.

Hannah dreaded what she knew would come later. When he had been drinking, it was all much worse. Then, there were no feelings at all, only pain. The intense pain that for him was inextricably linked to sexual pleasure.

"I have bought you a present." Anders opened a box and took out a black velvet bag. With a lustful look in his light blue eyes, he pulled a black leather mask out of the bag. He held it in his hand for a moment before dropping it on the floor. "You don't need a mask. I want to see the look in your eyes when you realize what's about to happen."

"Happen? What are you going to do to me?"

"The pain, you know, the greater the pain, the greater the pleasure." He reached into the bag and took out a small lacquer string and a naughty bra with chains. "What the hell?" He looked annoyed at the black g-string. "It claims to be bottomless. But the little hole in the bottom doesn't fit a big man like me. Well, fortunately I can do something about that." With his strong carpenter's hands, he tore the black panties, and the sound of the fabric being torn made Hannah shudder.

"What will you do to me?" she repeated, taking a step backwards.

"Come here, put the panties on." Hannah tried to cover her body but he pulled her hands away and handed her the g-string.

He watched her pulling them in place and then handed her the bra. "The chains will make sure your hands stay where they should be. I'm tired of you always trying to cover your breasts. They belong to me and I decide what happens to them."

A tear ran down Hannah's cheek as she closed the bra and adjusted the straps.

"Then place your hands in the chains." With a wicked grin, Anders pulled a flat whip out of the bag; a leather paddle with a carved heart in the middle.

"Now I'm going to give you a good spanking, so you can see how much I love you. You'll get big red hearts all over your body." Hannah screamed in fear, but Anders lit a cigarette and inhaled deeply before looking at Hannah thoughtfully.

As if in slow motion, she saw him stand up, and still holding the cigarette, he approached her.

"After pleasure, there will be pain, or is it the other way around? I think it's time to find out." With a swift movement, Anders pulled her bra aside and pressed the lit cigarette against her left breast.

Hannah sobbed in excruciating pain, begging, "Stop! Please don't hurt me."

Anders grinned and pressed the cigarette harder against her breast, and then for the first time in a long time, Hannah found her hiding place. It was like back in school when they teased her too much, but this time it was sheer terror that did the trick. At that precise moment, when the terror became too much for her to bear, she felt something moving inside her head. Something fluttered behind her eyes like the wings of a moth. It turned gray before her eyes as if she were in a fog bank. The fog grew denser, blotting out everything that could be seen and heard. The fog was a warm and safe place. No one could touch her there. The gray fog wrapped itself around her and protected her.

When she moved in with Anders, she had thought it would end her slide through the relentless currents. But she was wrong.

It would be a time of even more unpredictable currents and violent waterfalls, with no islands or sandbanks to give her a break. When he hadn't been drinking, he could be nice to her, but his mood swung as quickly as an April storm and it was impossible to predict what would trigger a tantrum.

Now, her life was marked with pain and even more isolation. She began to think that as much as she hated the isolation of her past life, at least there was no physical pain to accompany it. Now there was not only the pain of feeling unwanted and not worthy of love, but also the intense pain of mental and physical violence by someone who said he loved her.

"I'm so happy to have you here. I love the idea of you going to the apartment and waiting for me to come home." Anders stuck his hand down her panties and squeezed her buttocks on the way out the door.

Hannah had believed Anders when he said she could spend all the time she wanted drawing and painting, but that was not to be. During the many hours of the day when Anders was at work, she was alone. And in the first months, she had drawn a lot. There was no room for her easel, so she had just sat at the dining room table with her sketchpad and watercolors. But whenever Hannah showed Anders a finished drawing, he looked at it, turned it over, and told her how bad it was before tearing it up and setting fire to the pieces. After a while, she lost all desire to draw—the rejection was just too much. So, she sat apathetically watching the big TV until Anders came home. There was never any more talk of her going to art school after a gap year and Hannah herself had almost forgotten about it. It felt as if it was in a completely different life that she had drawn and painted and enjoyed it so much.

Hannah's father was as busy as ever, and her mother was utterly impossible. Every time they spoke on the phone, all her mother could talk about was how lucky Hannah was to have such a lovely boyfriend.

Hannah was not sure if luck was an apt description of her relationship with Anders. But she certainly wasn't alone anymore.

Every night, they lay close together on the narrow sofa bed, and when they went shopping, he always held her hand or had a strong arm around her back.

Hannah could clearly remember last Saturday when they had gone to the chemist for birth control pills as they did every three months, well before she had eaten the last pill in the package.

Anders had a firm grip on her hand and had pulled her so close to him that they looked like Siamese twins.

An elderly man stopped in front of them and stared at the tall young couple in surprised amazement. "I've never seen two men hold hands so openly!"

Anders turned angrily to the man. "That's a girl, you damn old fool." He slapped Hannah on the back of the head. "Duck when we're out together, I don't want you towering over me. You look like a fucking tranny!"

∿

"Come here." Anders smiled cruelly as he, for the twelfth time in just as many months, pushed her to the wall. "Now it's time. Time to stand against the wall!"

Hannah nodded but remained silent. Every first of the month, Anders demanded to measure her to see if she had grown.

He looked at his measuring stick. "You better fucking stop growing more. I'm six foot two, and I don't want a girlfriend taller than me..."

Hannah tried to make herself as small as possible. She had a feeling that she had grown quite a bit lately.

"Six feet, one point eight inches! Now you're stopping!" Without warning, he lashed out with the solid ruler in his hand, striking her hard across the groin.

Hannah's body convulsed in agony as she let out a piercing scream. Tears streamed down her face as she curled up into a ball, trying to shield herself from any further attacks. But the next thing that happened was Anders grabbing her arm and forcing her face into the carpet.

"Get down on the floor. Feel for yourself how much dirt is still there. You can't even vacuum properly. You're useless." He ran Hannah's right cheek back and forth against the hard pile of carpet.

Humiliation, condescension, and unworthiness were daily feelings for Hannah. But she put up with everything he did to her day after day.

The worst part was that he was always lovingly attentive when they visited her parents, which they did as rarely as possible, because Hannah had a clear memory of how her mother had hit on him. She remembered clearly the last time they had visited her parents, and Anders had smiled politely at her father and said:

"Your daughter is such a good housekeeper. She cooks delicious food, and she can cut my hair too. There's no end to what she can do. I love her beyond words. She is the love of my life." He sounded so convincing that even Hannah herself was about to believe it.

"Did Hannah cut your hair?" Hannah's mother let her hand slide over Anders' chic short haircut.

"Yeah, she's a great hairdresser." Anders hugged her, and Hannah gawked. Was this the same man who, just three days before, had scolded and stabbed her in the stomach with scissors because he wasn't happy with the result?

"I hope you know how lucky you are to have such a caring, stable, and loving boyfriend," Hannah's mother said, sounding envious as she watched her tall daughter in the arms of the handsome young man.

Chapter 6

The river grew narrower and wilder, but one of the trees on the bank stretched out its life-giving arms over the rushing stream and offered a brief respite until the violent waters uprooted the great tree and carried it downstream. Down towards a giant waterfall.

Anders grabbed his jacket and headed toward the door. "We'll have a guest today." Anders' voice slurred, and Hannah could see he had been drinking from the vodka bottle.

"A guest?" No one ever came for a visit. Not once in the year and a half she had lived in his apartment.

Anders continued, "My hopeless old father is coming around. He's an old idiot, and I fucking don't want to be around him today. I will go to the pub and have a drink or two. Just let him in and chat with him. Then call me when he's gone." Anders bolted out the door, leaving Hannah standing there, uncomprehending.

The doorbell rang, and Hannah scrambled, quickly kicking off her shoes so she was as short as possible, hastily running her fingers through her dark, shiny hair, taking a deep breath, and opening the door.

Outside stood a tall, middle-aged man who looked a lot like his son but had a gentle look in his eyes.

"Hi, nice to meet you. I'm Hugo." He gave Hannah a warm hug.

The simple touch felt like a punch in the belly. It was a feeling she had never experienced before. She didn't understand what was happening to her body. When Anders occasionally gave her a hug, she didn't react that way at all. She couldn't manage to say a single word. Her crotch grew hot, and she looked down at the floor, unable to meet his gaze. How could her body react like that to a man she had never met before? It was embarrassing. What if he told his son? She quickly squeezed her thighs together so that he didn't realize what was happening to her.

"It's been a long time since I've visited Anders. I've been working too hard since my wife died almost five years ago."

Hannah was about to fall over her own feet when she showed him into the living room and, without a word, pointed to the couch.

Anders' father smiled at her, and she met his calm eyes and couldn't help but return the smile. He sat in the middle of the couch, and Hannah took a deep breath and carefully sat on the edge.

"You are a beautiful girl; I hope my son treats you well." Hugo looked thoughtfully at the remains of a large bruise on Hannah's left cheek.

Hannah's eyes filled with tears, and she turned her face away.

"Look at me," Hugo said gently.

Hannah opened her eyes and met his searching look.

"Don't forget; I know my son."

Hannah's eyes darted nervously around the room as her father-in-law began to speak. She nodded along as he talked about his life as a traveling engineer, but she couldn't quite bring herself to speak.

"I know you're not married and you're not very old, so who knows what might happen in the future. But will it be all right if I call you daughter-in-law?"

Hannah nodded. Daughter-in-law. There was something sweet and reassuring about that word. Almost as if she really was his daughter.

"May I call you father-in-law, then?" She felt that warm feeling between her legs again. It was an adult feeling. A feeling that something could happen that could be fantastic. Something nice between a woman and a man. Something she had always longed to feel.

As the conversation continued, Hannah gradually began to relax, and she found herself drawn in by her father-in-law's stories of exotic locales and engineering challenges. She started asking questions, curious to learn more about his work and travels.

To her surprise, her father-in-law proved to be a good listener. He asked thoughtful questions about Hannah's interests and experiences, and she found herself opening up to him in ways she never had with anyone else. She confidently talked about her dreams of becoming a writer and her struggles to adapt to living in a small apartment in an entirely different part of the city. "I loved walking around in the old part of Copenhagen. There are so many interesting places."

"You don't do that anymore?"

Hannah shook her head without meeting Hugo's eyes. "Anders doesn't like to take walks. We just go shopping and return home straight away. Anders hates it when anyone thinks I'm a man because I'm so tall."

Her father-in-law burst into hearty laughter. A sound that made Hannah feel joy, not humiliation—a sound that promised more joy. It was a laugh that was infectious and so, she laughed with him.

As they talked, Hannah realized that he was a kind and intelligent man who had lived a rich and interesting life. And as the conversation drew to a close, she felt a sense of connection to him that she had never felt with anyone before.

Hannah paused and looked at the clock above the door. It was already seven o'clock. "I'm sorry, I've been talking for hours."

"You probably needed it." Her father-in-law patted her hand and cursed his son far into hell. "I feel like a knight from a fairy tale." Her father-in-law laughed a little uncertainly as he watched her expression change from astonishment to delight. "I want to free you from a golden tower or rescue you from a fire-breathing dragon."

"I'm not sure I understand what you mean." Hannah's voice was uncertain, but as he kept looking at her, she suddenly realized that she felt the same way about him. She felt a deep desire to do something for him.

"I know I mustn't, that it's strictly forbidden, but I want to hold you so much. Just this once and then never again. Tomorrow I have to leave and be away for several weeks."

Hannah tilted her head back a bit and rested it on his shoulder. Sitting so close to him was torture, but it wasn't easy to tear herself away when she knew it would be the last time they would sit so close. The feelings she could feel flutter in her chest must be repressed, though she was desperate for a caring human connection.

He saw her beautiful young face, which, after their long conversation, had taken on an inner glow that was indescribably lovely. Her father-in-law tried to withdraw, but invisible chains held him tight, close to her warm body. What the hell had gotten into him? A small moan escaped him, and he pressed her to him in a big bear hug.

"Little sweet girl, why didn't I meet you first," he murmured, "then a lot would have been different."

Hannah felt an indescribable warmth spread from her toes to her head. She opened her mouth to say something, but at once, her father-in-law pressed his warm lips against hers. Very gently at first, but as she opened her mouth even more and hungrily returned his kiss, it became more violent and demanding.

They both forgot everything around them. The only thing that mattered was that they were sitting close together, pressed against each other and with their lips open so their tongues could explore and claim. Hannah felt her stiff nipples pressing against his chest, and a distinct bulge in his pants showed her how much he desired her.

She needed tenderness and compassion and she suddenly felt desperate to feel his warm arms around her body. She didn't want him to leave. He had to stay with her. It was the only thought there was room for in her head. "Stay with me," she murmured.

"It's no good, little girl, we can't do this."

She could tell he was struggling with what was right and what they both needed. But suddenly Hugo pulled back and looked deep into her eyes before, with an animal sound, he grabbed and showered her with kisses. He pulled her up from the couch, and their bodies pressed close together. Hannah could feel the hard erection against her crotch.

Slowly her father-in-law unbuttoned the top buttons of her blouse, and suddenly he stood with a firm young breast in his hand.

Hannah had not heard the door open but saw the empty vodka bottle being smashed into her father-in-law's head just before Anders slapped her in the face, wild with rage.

"What the fuck happens in my house when I'm gone for a minute?" Anders was furious.

"Nothing happened." Her father-in-law tried to intervene, but Anders struck him in the head again, this time so hard that the bottle broke, and blood began to run down his father's face and onto the floor, where it formed a large sticky red pool of blood. Anders pushed him out the door and slammed it shut behind him. "You fucking bitch, what the fuck do you think you're doing?" Anders slapped Hannah again and looked at her with a wicked smile.

She slumped to the floor. The gray fog of fear was about to overtake her.

"So, you're into old men? Big old cocks. But you'll have to settle for my big cock. You're mine, and from now on, you won't be allowed to leave the apartment, and you won't be allowed to let anyone in, either. You're mine, and you're staying here with me! It's only my cock you're going to play with!" Anders' voice was sharp as he continued. "Are you wearing the underwear I gave you?"

She didn't look at him. "No."

"Why not? Didn't I tell you to always put it on when I'm home?"

"I didn't feel like it today..."

"You should have worn it." His voice was calm, but his eyes had a dangerous gleam.

Hannah walked over to the dresser and picked up a set of black lacquer underwear and stepped toward the bathroom.

"I want you to stay here." He tugged brutally on her arm. "I need you to put the clothes on in front of me."

Hannah didn't move.

He raised his hand threateningly.

She turned her back to him and began unbuttoning her blouse. "Turn around and look at me!" he commanded.

Hannah met Anders' gaze briefly before looking down again and, with fumbling fingers, unbuttoned the last buttons and pulled off her blouse. The firm young breasts were strutting, and she was ashamed of her body's reaction. Quickly she pulled the black lacquer bra on and adjusted the chains on the bra so that her breasts were stretched as high up and close together as possible. Hannah left the fastened chains hanging and quickly stepped out of her pants and panties at once before sticking her legs into the little naughty lacquer g-string and pulling it up, so it just covered the dark curls. She stood before him, eyes downcast.

"Look at me." Anders was rubbing his cock to make it hard and ready. "Now put the chains on..."

Hannah attached the chains from the bra to the panties and thrust her hands into the open loops.

"Kneel in front of me and spread your legs," he commanded.

Automatically she knelt in front of him and spread her legs as wide as possible, but when Hannah saw his dark look of danger, she tried to bring her hands down to cover herself. But the chains prevented her from doing so, and with a sigh, she opened her mouth, ready to receive what she knew was coming.

Anders slapped her hands away. "I didn't give you permission to do that. You have a big, disgusting pussy filled with long hair. Haven't I told you over and over again that you must shave it, so I feel invited?" He shoved the big red cock right in her face.

Hannah got tears in her eyes and bit her lips hard together.

"I want to choke you with it." Brutally, Anders thrust the cock deep into her mouth and laughed as she began to emit vomiting sounds. "Fucking suck it; you love that cock. Now come on and give me what I want." He slapped her hard in the crotch and pinched her nipple.

She was choking and started to gasp when he suddenly let out a roar and filled her mouth with his hot cum.

He stood up and, with a quick movement, tilted his cock back into his pants, leaving her lying on the floor crying.

She lay on the floor sobbing for a long time before she got up with difficulty and tore off the sticky cloth, spitting the last remnants of his semen onto the floor.

"Damn it, you fucking bitch, didn't I tell you to swallow?"

Chapter 7

The thunder of the enormous waterfall ahead roared and roared, and the river carried its prey over the edge of the raging waterfall, throwing tons of water and trying to force it below the surface.

Since her father-in-law's visit, Hannah had only seen Anders. He went to work and returned home, leaving her alone in the apartment. The door was always locked and could only be opened from the outside with the key. The key which Anders made sure to bring with him every morning. When she spoke with her parents on the phone, Anders sat beside her and monitored every word.

They went shopping together, and every time Hannah ate, she went to the toilet and threw up. Always as quietly as possible so Anders wouldn't suspect. That was the only way she could be sure he wouldn't use it against her.

She became weaker and number as time passed, and she lost more and more weight. Her common sense told her it was wrong, but she no longer cared. She no longer wanted to live. She was trapped and desperately wanted this nightmare to be over. Until the day she threw up one morning BEFORE she had eaten breakfast.

She dragged herself out of bed and into the bathroom. Something was off. Her body felt like it was working against her. She wondered if it could be the stomach flu?

But no, it continued for the next few days, and Hannah became more and more debilitated and felt more tired than ever before.

"Get me a beer," Anders commanded from the couch, turning on the television.

Hannah fetched a beer from the fridge and handed it to him. As they watched a young girl singing on stage, Anders took a swig of his beer and commented, "Look at that fat bitch. She looks like she's about to burst. How the fuck can they let a pregnant bitch go on stage? That's fucking disgusting."

Pregnant? Hannah felt like everything was spinning and all she wanted was to throw herself on the floor and scream. Was that what was wrong with her? Could she be pregnant despite being on the pill? She needed to take a pregnancy test, but how? She had no money and couldn't leave the apartment without Anders.

Thinking quickly, Hannah forced a smile and told Anders that they needed to go to the pharmacy the next day because she had run out of pills. Angered by her apparent carelessness, Anders shook her by the hair, but ultimately agreed to take her to the pharmacy.

Desperate to find out if she was pregnant, Hannah tried to come up with a plan. But she was petrified. Could she fool Anders? And then, what if she was? What would she do? How was she going to raise a child? A feeling of dread surged through her and began to fill her up when another thought suddenly crept into her head. If she was pregnant, she would have a child she could love and who would love her. And it was exactly what she had always dreamed of. It was time for her to pull herself together and be strong and act like an adult, even though she was not eighteen. When they were at the pharmacy, Anders always used to stand and stare at the condoms. He rarely went to the cash register but would give Hannah money to buy the pills. Before they went to the pharmacy, she slipped the old packet of pills into her pocket. At the cash register, she hurriedly glanced at Anders, who, just as she had expected, stood grinning as he looked at the condoms.

"All these condoms are way too small for me." Anders grinned cheekily at a young lady standing and looking at sanitary napkins. Hannah gave the clerk a pale smile and grabbed one of the pregnancy tests that were thankfully still in a pile right by the cash register where she had noticed them when she bought the pills last time. Hannah quickly put the pregnancy test in her pocket and returned to Anders with the old packet of pills in her hand.

⁂

"Open the pack, pee on the tip, wait five minutes, then check for one or two streaks," Hannah muttered the following day when Anders had left, and she was all alone in the apartment. It was Friday, and Anders would probably not be home until late. Almost every Friday, he went out with his friends. If she was lucky, he was so drunk when he got home that he fell asleep immediately. If not, it was the worst day of the week. The day he was extra inventive and violent and unpleasant. The hot stream hit the tip of the pregnancy test, and a few hot drops of urine hit her hand, making her shiver. "Please let me not be pregnant." Hannah repeated the words over and over again while waiting for the minutes to pass away.

"FUCK, fuck, and more fuck," Hannah sobbed and sank onto the bathroom floor. There were two lines on the test. Did she deserve that too? Hadn't she suffered enough? She remembered the words Anders always said: "After joy, the pain will come; without pain, no pleasure." She had had her pleasure. Those few hours with her father-in-law had been some of the best hours of her life. So now comes the pain.

The doorbell rang, and Hannah scrambled. She wondered who it could be? No one ever came there. She stared at the locked door and sighed. She couldn't even let anyone in because the door was locked from the outside and Anders had the only key. She murmured to herself, *"I hope it is not someone who wants to hurt me. I have a child to take care of now."*

A thought suddenly filled her head. Hurt her? Who would ring the doorbell to hurt her? She waited in front of the door but nobody knocked. It was probably just someone who had pressed the wrong button. A thought suddenly popped into her head. There was no one but Anders that hurt her. And he did it because she allowed him to. He did it because she hadn't been able to stop it. It was her own fault. In a not-too-distant future, she would turn eighteen. Then she would be an adult. She thought perhaps it was time she started acting like an adult—an adult who was soon to be a mother!

Hannah put her hands on her stomach. She had already come to love this child in just a few hours. She would protect her baby and provide all the love, care, protection, and attention she never got. She would treat the child very differently than her parents had treated her. And above all, she would always have time for her child. A whole new feeling, a feeling of euphoria, seized her. At that moment, the sum of the positive emotions was more significant than the sum of the negative ones. Whenever she thought positive thoughts, she remembered her old math teacher. She silently sent him a loving thought. And when she did a simple calculation and subtracted the negative result from the positive, the result was positive! In other words, she felt genuinely happy!

"Don't be afraid, little darling. Nothing's going to happen," she whispered to her stomach. She now had a new life in her belly, utterly dependent on her, depending on her to show courage and action and not, as so many times before, stand by and put up with being beaten and humiliated.

Hannah's stomach churned, and a bout of nausea made her cringe. She wrapped her arms around her stomach and bowed her head. "Don't worry, little darling; Mummy will look after you." Even if it was the last thing she did, she had to show her unborn child she wasn't afraid. Hannah repeated, "Don't worry, everything will be all right." She gently let her hand slide down over her still-flat belly. Fortunately, Anders had no idea she was pregnant. Her hopelessly lousy habit of eating and then throwing up meant she was still slim. Suddenly, a terrifying thought struck her.

If Anders discovered she was pregnant, would he even believe he was the child's father? Could he get the idea that his father had made her pregnant? Hannah shivered and pressed her arms tighter around her stomach. Would Anders believe her when she told him there had never been more between her and her father-in-law than a kiss and a hug? Anders most certainly would not, and it was entirely her fault. It was her fault for having stood in her father-in-law's arms and, for a weak moment, turned her face to his, and enjoyed a gentle and loving kiss. Anders would never believe that it was his child. Not when he had seen the look on her face when she looked at her father-in-law. As close a feeling to love as she had ever known had been in her eyes and in his too—after only a few hours.

No, there was nothing to do but to get away, away from Anders—far away, so she could give birth to her child and be safe. Hannah poured herself a glass of water but didn't have time to drink it before another thought occurred. She was all alone in the apartment. Anders wouldn't be home until late. The door was, of course, locked from the outside. But she could open the window and climb down the wall. The apartment was only on the first floor, and the ivy growing up the wall would support her. Even though she was so tall, she was still thin. She had to get away. Away right now. It was her only chance.

Suddenly determined and active, she began rummaging in her closet. She needed warm, dark, practical clothes, and flat boots. Then, she needed the money she'd secretly saved up over the last few months. It wasn't much, but enough to get her far away from Anders. Where she should go, she wasn't sure. But she had to get away. Now! That, she knew. She opened the window and stuck one leg out over the cornice, grabbing the sturdy creeper that covered the entire wall, and was about to let the other leg follow when a pair of strong hands grabbed tightly around her neck and pulled her back into the small apartment where she had spent so many agonizing and miserable hours.

"Where the hell do you think you're going? What are you doing, you filthy bitch?"

The sensation of Anders' brutal fingers around her neck was indescribably disgusting, and she gasped and tried to wriggle free.

"What the fuck is that?" Anders released her with one hand, and with the other, he reached for the white plastic rod lying on the windowsill. "What the hell? Two lines! Are you fucking pregnant, you horny little bitch?" He tightened his grip around her neck. "Fucking bitch!" He continued, "And since you were about to run away from me, there's no doubt who the kid's father is. Who else but the old bastard I've had the misfortune to have as a father."

Hannah drew in a sharp breath and sobbed. "It is not his child. We haven't done anything. Your father would never touch me. You have to believe me." Hannah was crying openly now. "Your father is a good man."

"Good man! Ha, yeah, good at making children pregnant. That'll be a fucking lie. Now I'll fucking kill him and the kid too."

For the first time, Hannah realized that Anders was mentally ill. She realized it wasn't just because he'd been drinking; something was wrong in his head. And most importantly, she realized it wasn't her fault at all, and she would never be able to change it.

"I'm not having a fucking baby. And definitely not someone else's baby." Anders dragged Hannah out the door and down the stairs. And only his firm grip on her arm prevented her from falling. With his other hand, he grabbed her hair and forced her head upwards, nodding her nose, making it bleed.

"I'm sorry, I know it was wrong of me. But your father was just being kind and friendly." She tried to wipe the blood off her nose with her sleeve.

"I'll show you what I do to that old bastard. I'll fucking kill him." Anders was furious.

Hannah was terrified, hugging her stomach as she tried to stay upright. "Please, let's go back to the apartment." Anders hesitated for a second, and Hannah continued with a pleading voice. "Then I'll do anything you want…"

"No, there will be time for some fun later. Now we're going on a picnic. The old man lives all alone in the middle of the forest." He laughed wickedly and continued, "And when I have dealt with my father, it's your turn." He tore open the car door and threw Hannah into the front seat.

The familiar gray fog began to settle over her, but a flickering spark suddenly lit as she thought of the baby. She couldn't stay silent and still any longer. She had to fight the fog, if not for herself, then for her baby. Hannah woke abruptly from her gray trance. She couldn't allow anything to happen to the baby. She had to be strong.

"Don't be afraid, little one; nothing will happen." Hannah's voice sounded slightly desperate as she whispered soothingly to her unborn child. She needed a miracle now, but it was probably too much to hope for because she wasn't used to miracles. "Nothing is happening," she repeated. Perhaps her unborn child did not need reassurance, but she did.

Anders let the cigarette he was smoking dangle between his lips as he roared through the town and continued down the highway, squeezing his eyes against the cigarette smoke that filled the cabin and made Hannah cough.

Hannah knew that her father-in-law lived in a small house in the country near one of Denmark's largest forests. A lovely, peaceful place where birds soared and deer roamed freely. Hannah sincerely hoped he wasn't home. She hoped that he was still traveling. She couldn't bear to be the cause of anything happening to him.

Suddenly, Anders took his hand off the wheel long enough to reach out and rip her blouse open. He then took his lit cigarette out of his mouth and pressed the glowing tip against her exposed breast.

Hannah screamed in pain and once again felt the gray fog begin to descend over her. And once again, only the thought of the baby in her belly kept her from diving into oblivion.

Anders grinned wickedly at her distress and threw the flattened cigarette onto the backseat. With his hand now free, he reached into the glove compartment and pulled out a large serrated knife.

Hannah froze as she felt the cold metal of the knife press against the skin of her left breast. Her heart pounded in her chest as she let out a startled howl, the sound echoing through the small car.

The gray fog descended over her despite her best efforts to maintain control. She felt like she was sinking deep below the surface of the river, unable to stay afloat. But from her innermost resources, resources she had not known she possessed until that moment, she forced herself to stay focused. She knew from bitter experience that the more she screamed, the more violent he became. So she gritted her teeth and kept control of her shaking body.

The car skidded on the empty forest road as Anders grinned at her, a sickening smile that sent shivers down her spine. While driving with his left hand, he held the knife steady, with his right, the tip still pressed against her left breast.

Hannah's mind raced as she tried to think of a way out of this mess. And as she looked into Anders' eyes, she saw something that made her blood run cold. There was a gleam of madness in his gaze, a sense of pure malevolence that made her realize just how much danger she was in. She wondered how she had not seen it before. It was only now with this incredible instinct to protect her unborn child that she saw how sick this man really was.

With a sudden surge of strength, Hannah twisted her body, trying to break free of his grasp. But he was too strong, and he held her in place, the knife still pressed against her chest.

"What do you think the old man will say when you only have one breast left?" Anders pressed the knife harder against the soft, white skin, nearly penetrating it at its tip. "Do you think he still want to fuck you when your tits aren't there anymore?" The sharp knife cut a deep gash in her left breast and the warm blood dripped down her stomach.

The narrow, winding road through the woods was dark and somewhat foggy. A deer suddenly ran across the road right before them and grazed the bumper before disappearing into the woods.

"Fuck!" Anders had to let go of Hannah's arm and keep both hands on the steering wheel to straighten the car.

The collision with the big animal sent her hurtling toward the door. The seat belt tightened around her chest, making her scream in pain, and her right hand automatically grabbed the door handle.

Hannah suddenly knew this was her only chance to escape Anders. Her only chance to get away from a crazy man who wanted to kill her and her unborn child. She simultaneously pressed the button that released her seat belt with her left hand while she struggled to open the car door with her right hand.

Anders released the steering wheel with both hands trying to stop her. "Where the hell do you think you're going?" He groped frantically for her arm.

Seconds after Hannah had thought for the first time in her life how amazing it was to have long arms, her elbow was in the middle of Anders' face. He cursed her in hell, as blood flowed violently from his nose.

He jerked the accelerator to the floor and screamed like a maniac as the car skidded into the opposite lane and threw Hannah out the door that was partially opened.

The last thing she saw before rolling down the slope on the side of the road was the white light from the headlights of the oncoming truck suddenly appearing out of the fog. The sound of the truck's violent honk and the ensuing loud crash as the two cars collided head-on lingered in her ears long after she rolled to the ditch's bottom, dragging a mass of branches and withered leaves with her.

Hannah lay perfectly still under the dead branches—half in her fog, half in shock. The noise of sirens and voices drifted down to her, but she stayed in her hiding place. Only long after all sounds had disappeared and the silence on the narrow forest road had settled again, Hannah moved her bruised and battered body. She wept with pain, cold, and exhaustion, but at the same time, a strange feeling of relief filled her.

A sharp pain was passing through her abdomen, and she moaned loudly. *Oh, no, please no, not the baby. Haven't I been through enough?* Hannah screamed in agonizing pain, pushed the branches and leaves away, and crawled to the nearest tree trunk. She grabbed the rough trunk, and by leaning on it, she managed to get to her feet. She stood swaying there momentarily, bruised and bloodied, trying to make her broken body feel better. Suddenly she was overcome by overwhelming guilt. She had killed her child…

Hannah released her grip on the tree trunk and half staggered, half scrambled up the slope, where she fell over on the roadside, unable to hold herself upright any longer.

Through the hell of pain, broken fragments of her past emerged. She lost consciousness and collapsed on the roadside.

Chapter 8

A short distance into the horizon, a sandbank suddenly appeared, a sandbank of the most beautiful white sand, a place inviting to rest.

Virginia quietly opened the door to the hospital room and looked at Hannah, who was in a restless sleep and obviously dreaming. She smiled lovingly at the sleeping young girl, whom she had seen for the first time the day before, and began humming a gentle little lullaby.

Through the mist of dreams, Hannah realized that the same gentle and loving voice that had brought her back to life the last time she dreamed had returned. The loving voice hummed softly, and Hannah forced her eyes open. And sure enough, the kind, unknown lady who had told her that her name was Virginia was once again sitting beside her bed. Hannah's eyes closed again, and Virginia's gentle voice reminded her of a perfect day she had in sixth grade. The only perfect day of her life so far. The day when Henry kissed her and treated her with milk chocolate. The day she felt like a normal girl being admired by a boy. Hannah moaned in pain, and the boy disappeared from her thoughts, despite her desperate attempts to keep him there. Hannah screamed in her sleep and slowly regained consciousness. She blinked her eyes many times and tried to open them but gave up; the effort was too great.

"I don't want to live a life in fear. I will not submit to your vicious desires. Leave me alone."

She cried and returned to the dark river that engulfed her and brought her oblivion. She felt herself being carried away by the waters, drowning in pain. And the familiar gray fog was about to engulf her, but Virginia's cool hand on her forehead energized her. Hannah forced her eyes open and met Virginia's happy, smiling gaze.

"Wake up, my sweet girl, you're dreaming." Virginia stroked her hair with loving care. "You've slept all through the night, so now you've been in the hospital for six days."

"Six days ... then it was yesterday that I saw you for the first time?"

Virginia nodded and stroked her hair gently.

Hannah murmured, "I had a lot of strange dreams and it was like my whole life was flashing before my eyes. It was very scary."

Virginia nodded. "Yes, it must have been very traumatizing to relive it all. But I've been watching you while you were dreaming, and I can see that you can disappear from the world around you." Virginia caressed her cheek. "I can understand why, and it was certainly the best thing you could do at the time. But now you have other options."

"Options? I don't understand." Hannah noticed a strange and unfamiliar warm feeling in her body. A feeling that something positive and wonderful was about to happen.

"You must never let the darkness take over. Every time you feel the darkness about to settle over your mind, you must counter it."

"How do I do that?"

"You have to find a memory that is so good and strong that it can fill you up completely with positive thoughts. You need to hold that thought in you for as long as possible. Once you learn how to hold the thought, you'll never have to fear the fog taking over again."

Hannah nodded, and Virginia took her hand and held it.

"What are you afraid of, my sweet girl?" Virginia asked.

"Anders..."

"Tell me a little about your life with Anders." Virginia momentarily moved her eyes away from Hannah and down to her handbag, where a five-day-old newspaper with a picture of a smashed-up car was visible.

"Anders..." Hannah hesitated. "What do you want to know about him?" Her expression shifted, and she was unwilling to meet Virginia's eyes.

Virginia could clearly see the look of sheer terror through Hannah's beautiful features.

Hannah felt the familiar gray fog gather in her head, but before she sank into its soft depths, a gentle and loving kiss on the forehead made her open her eyes again.

"The past must never have power over the future. Anders isn't here anymore. He's dead and gone now and can't hurt you anymore. Now you must think ahead. When fear knocks, and it will do so many times in your life, it must always be your faith that opens the door; never fear. When you remember that, everything will be much easier to handle."

"The time with Anders was so horrible," Hannah sobbed uncontrollably. "I can't understand how I let Anders do these things to me. I must be a very weak person."

"It's over, and we're moving on now. Let's not dwell on the past. Remember that you can't change the past; you can only learn from it. It's your future you can do something about." Virginia smiled softly at Hannah. "But now you're awake and it's time to eat. I have brought you a nice homemade lunch." Virginia handed Hannah some delicious chicken salad and a piece of home-baked bread. "It's important that you remember to eat. You have to take care of yourself." Virginia looked at her wristwatch and rose from the chair. "Try to get some more sleep. I'll be back tomorrow."

⁂

Now that Hannah was feeling better, she was ready to have visitors. Every time there was visiting time, she peeked out into the hallway, hoping that her parents would come and see her. For some reason she didn't understand and hadn't yet dared to ask, Virginia never came by during visiting hours.

Virginia sat there very often when Hannah was waking from her nap and again after supper, but never during the two times a day when someone else might drop by. A light knock roused Hannah from her sad thoughts, and she turned her head toward the doorway.

"Hmmm ... I hope you are feeling better..." Her distracted and indifferent father stood leaning against the doorframe, looking like he'd rather be anywhere but in the hospital with his only daughter.

"Your things are at my office." Hannah's father looked at his watch. "You can pick them up when you're ready."

"Pick up? I thought I would be staying with you and Mom?"

"No, you can't. You know I'm busy. The magazine has to be published ... and there's all the other stuff..."

Yes, Hannah knew very well what "other stuff" stood for. Ladies! Apparently, he was still fooling around.

Her father hesitated for a moment before he continued, "Your mother and I are getting divorced, and I'm moving into a smaller apartment, and your mother is probably moving abroad with her latest boyfriend. She was talking about Switzerland."

Hannah glared at her father. "What am I going to do?" She let out a small, almost silent fart. "Where am I going to live?"

"You'll be eighteen soon, but until then, I have found a solution." Her father smiled one of his rare smiles and took a large white envelope out of his pocket. "Here, take this," he said. He was at the bedside table in two leaps, placing the envelope on top of the brochure on eating disorders that a nurse had brought in earlier. "I think you'll like it." He stepped quickly back to the safety of the doorway.

Hannah had never seen her father show emotion, and there was no sign of it now.

"Aren't you going to open it?" He cast another stolen glance at his watch, but not quick enough for Hannah to miss it.

Hannah slowly reached out and took the large envelope, an intriguing, brightly colored folder, a plane ticket, and a thick stack of dollar bills. She looked in the envelope a second time, but there was no letter inside, and before she could ask her father what the meaning was, he waved at her.

"I must go now. I hope you'll enjoy your stay. Six months on an excellent art course in New York. You've always been so fond of art and painting, and I thought it would be good for you to get away for a while."

Hannah moved her eyes from the empty doorway and began to read the leaflet. It sounded exciting. And her father was right. After all, she loved to draw and paint and missed it so much. Maybe it would be good to get away from everything, too. She'd try talking to Virginia about it and hear what she thought about it all.

"Oops, I almost forgot." Her father tossed a cell phone onto her bed. "I bought you a phone. Now we can always reach you."

Its irony was not lost on her. She let out a cynical sneer and muttered to herself—*Spend time talking to me? Yes, that's right.* Whenever she tried to talk to them, they were too preoccupied with their own lives to even acknowledge her presence. And even when they were physically present, they were emotionally distant, engrossed in their gadgets and unaware of her existence. But now she had given up. She had realized that their love and attention would never come, and she had long since stopped trying to break through the wall her parents had built, realizing that it was a futile exercise. And the thought of subjecting herself to yet more rejection and disappointment was unbearable.

Every day for the next five days, Virginia came and sat by her bedside. And every day, Hannah told her a little more about her life. But even though she already cared deeply for Virginia, she still held back the most horrible memories. She had decided never again to think about the child she had lost. There was no point in talking about it when it was her fault anyway. It was much better just to try to forget about it all, and just talk about all the things she liked to do. She told her about her love of reading and how she loved to find interesting quotes, which she paraphrased and kept in one of her many notebooks. She talked about her passion for painting and her love for Copenhagen's old town and the beautiful, peaceful parks. Through it all, Virginia listened attentively and gave her a much-needed sense of validation and support.

More than once, Hannah saw an expression in Virginia's eyes that clearly said that she knew there was something Hannah was hiding, and Hannah hastily changed the subject and asked, "What do you think of this drawing?" Hannah opened her yellow notebook and showed Virginia a sketch of an old farmhouse. "Does this look like the farm where you live?"

Virginia smiled and let out a little fart. "Yes, my sweet girl, but let's talk about you instead."

It suddenly occurred to Hannah that Virginia didn't talk about herself very much. Virginia listened far more than she spoke.

Anyway, it probably didn't matter. Hannah suddenly came to think of something. "Mom sent me a text."

"A text?" Virginia thoughtfully removed a U-shaped hairpin, straightened the shape, and aligned it better.

"Yes, a short text, of course. Mom was busy."

"Was she indeed?" A rare look of anger spread across Virginia's usually gentle face.

Hannah nodded. "Mother was on her way to Hawaii with her boyfriend," she said. "She was hoping they could get married on the beach." Hannah sighed profoundly and fervently, refusing to meet Virginia's gaze.

Virginia took the bull by the horns. "You'll be ready to go home soon."

Hannah would not meet Virginia's gaze. "I don't have a home anymore."

"What about the apartment you've been living in with Anders?"

"It wasn't a home, it was hell, and there's no way I'm going back there."

"Where do you want to go? Is there somewhere, in particular, you'd like to call home?"

Hannah shook her head. "Nah, there's nowhere I want to be, and Dad's decided I'm going to New York anyway."

"New York? What are you going to do there?"

"Go to an art class." Hannah held the folder out to Virginia, who pretended not to see it.

"Would you like that?"

"Well…" Hannah closed her eyes and considered. "After all, I love to draw and paint, and it's one of the things I know I can do well." She continued thoughtfully, "And it's something my dad thought would be good for me, so I'd like to try. I want to get away from it all, and New York is a big city, so hopefully I can have some peace there. I don't know why he chose a school as far away as New York, but it suits me fine. The farther away, the better." She didn't even admit to herself that she wanted to escape from her own heavy thoughts about the accident and her miscarriage and the lack of people loving her.

For a moment, Virginia looked like she was going to say something—something important, something Hannah wouldn't like to hear. But instead, she stood up, turned away from the tall, beautiful girl in the bed, and tried to hide, wiping a tear from her cheek.

"I'm going to miss you." Hannah sighed deeply. "You've made me feel safe. I don't know how I'll manage on my own."

"When you believe, you'll find the way no matter what. And now I will wish you an amazing trip, my sweet girl." Virginia handed her a neatly folded piece of paper. "My address, in case you ever want to come and visit me at my farm by the North Sea." Virginia walked to the door and looked at Hannah with a gentle and loving smile as she said:

>"When we begin to live a life
>from the heart
>without filter
>much will fall away.
>
>We move to the next level
>by saying no
>to things we could do
>that don't resonate anymore
>and saying yes
>to a period
>without a view."

Virginia sent her a finger kiss. "Living from your heart is exactly what you're going to do now. I wish you all the best and hope to see you again someday. Go out into the world. Become *someone* and come back and become *something!*"

Chapter 9

The river had leveled out and become shallow, creating a wading pool that provided new opportunities to fortify themselves for what lay ahead.

"The Farm on The Edge of The World," Hannah muttered as she struggled to get herself and her bags safely down from the dusty platform located in the northernmost part of Denmark, close to the North Sea, the part of Denmark where Virginia lived on her farm. In the few short weeks she had been at the school in New York and until now when she was back in Denmark, so much had happened.

"I am waiting for you, for as long as it takes. When you're ready, just take the train to my farm. No need to call first; I'll be home when you get there." That was the last thing Virginia had said while Hannah was still in the hospital.

Hannah sighed. She felt several years older. Of course, she was older, too, eighteen now, because it had just been her birthday. She was finally an adult and could make her own decisions.

The train stopped at the platform, and Hannah gathered her things. She didn't have to hurry because that was the end of the line. She was as far west as she could get.

Only two other passengers got off, and they hurried toward the small grocery store on the other side of the platform.

Hannah settled her backpack to avoid the straps hurting her recently healed wounds and picked up the two suitcases. A strange feeling spread through her—a feeling she didn't know. It was the first entirely positive feeling she had had since the accident. She took a deep breath and felt it again. It was a good feeling—a feeling of being on the way home. How could that be? She was on her way to a totally unknown place—a place that was very far from anything she knew, a place where she knew only one person, and even that person she had only known for a short time.

The sun was low in the sky. It was January, so it would not be long before it set. Hannah let her eyes drift around the horizon—water, forest, sky, sand, and stone. She realized the dusty look came from the beautiful white sand carried into the air by the strong wind. She raised her hands above her head and tried to catch the grains of sand. She felt hints of fear flutter nervously in her chest. She stopped and let the feeling take over. Yes, it was definitely fear, but a different kind of fear than the one she'd felt when Anders pulled her into the car and sped up, and she could see the truck towering in front of them. A different kind of fear than she had felt in the hospital. This was just the fear of the unknown—not an all-consuming fear that couldn't be controlled.

A lone taxi pulled up next to the small grocery store, and Hannah walked toward it.

༺

"The Farm on The Edge of The World!" Hannah whispered, standing still in the middle of the courtyard before she gathered enough courage and knocked on the low door of the main building.

"Nay, what beholds my eye!" Virginia exclaimed, presenting Hannah with a huge burst of delight. "Well, this is a pleasant surprise!" Hannah ran into her warm and gentle hug. "I'm so happy you've come! It must be a belated birthday present."

"Has it just been your birthday?" Hannah felt the same calmness spread through her body that she had felt those days in the hospital and began to think she had made the right decision by traveling west to an unfamiliar little town on the North Sea.

"Yes, on the seventh of January. I turned fifty-six." Virginia answered Hannah's unspoken question with a smile.

"Congratulations." Hannah looked down at the gravel, at the large yard between the barns.

"Are you here to stay?" Virginia looked appraisingly at the two suitcases Hannah had set down in the yard.

"I don't know if you want me here. After all, I'm almost a stranger to you. We only spent a short time talking when I was still at the hospital." Hannah dared not meet Virginia's eyes.

"Of course, I want you, my sweet girl. Why wouldn't I?"

Hannah blushed and murmured, "I didn't turn into 'somebody' like you said I should. I tried, but it didn't work at all."

"Don't worry. We'll do something about that later. Once you become SOMEBODY, you find your own way and become SOMETHING. That's just the way it is. But come along and let me show you around The Farm on The Edge of The World."

"You're so sweet. I'm so glad I plucked up the courage to come over here."

"I am so happy that you came. You can place your things here." Virginia opened a low door into the main house. "Mind your head, my sweet girl. The farm dates back to 1785; people were small then, and you must bow your head. Fortunately, I'm not that old, but I'm just as small."

Hannah smiled and looked down at the little woman in the funny flowered dress. A woman she had only known for a short time but who already meant more to her than any other human ever had. Hannah would never forget her kind words and soothing touch during all her days in the hospital. She wondered how a stranger could be so caring toward her when the people who were supposed to love her most didn't seem to care at all.

Virginia noticed Hannah's wonder at her attire. "I feel comfortable in loose patterned dresses. To me, they signal casualness and love. But luckily, we are all different." She looked at Hannah's too-short jeans and the white blouse that dulled at the sleeves. "If I had a sewing machine … and if I knew how to sew, I'd make you something long enough. Luckily, I know a lady who can sew, so we'll get you something that fits. That lady sews some of my dresses too."

"Those dresses look great on you, but I'd feel all wrong in clothes like that."

"That's quite all right, my sweet girl. We all have to be different. And besides, you look lovely. You must find your own style. Exactly what you feel comfortable in."

"I love strong colors, but the patterns and composition should exude calmness. I like to mix strong colors with basic colors, black, or white."

"That's the artist talking, I hear." Virginia smiled happily. "I'm looking forward to seeing you paint. By the way, there is an empty room in the other building. You're welcome to it if you'd like to use it as your art studio."

"That's really nice of you; I'd love to." Hannah suddenly felt the need to use the restroom. "Can I use the toilet?"

"Sure, it's right here, but watch your head…" Virginia went ahead and turned on the light.

"Oops." Hannah had forgotten that the doorway wasn't built for a modern person at well over six feet tall.

"That won't be the last time you hit your head," Virginia said, turning her back to open the refrigerator.

A distinct thump from the bathroom told Virginia that Hannah had, once again, forgotten to account for the fact that the exposed beams were not much more than five and a half feet above the floor level. Hannah came out of the bathroom rubbing her head.

"I forgot to be careful." Hannah looked embarrassed and continued, "And the toilet was so low, it was difficult getting up. I had to make several attempts." She looked at Virginia, who was whipping cream at the table. "The kitchen table is very low too." Hannah positioned herself in front of it, and sure enough, it only went just above her knee.

"The table fits me well, but we must do something about it, so you can use it without getting a sore back," Virginia said with care.

"Are you making a cake?" Hannah watched curiously as Virginia quickly and deftly filled the cake base with cream and arranged it on a platter along with the candied peaches.

"Yes, you deserve a cake, my sweet girl." Virginia placed the almost finished birthday cake on a platter and gave the young girl a beaming smile. Hannah's heart swelled with gratitude to the tiny woman who had made her a birthday cake. As she looked at the cake in front of her, Hannah couldn't help but feel a sense of joy mixed with sadness. She had hoped that her parents would be there to celebrate this special day with her, but as usual, they were too busy with their own lives to remember.

Virginia looked at her with a smile, and Hannah thought she had never felt as loved and appreciated as she did in that moment. She gave Virginia a big hug, unable to say a word, but felt the warmth of Virginia's embrace and the genuine care in her heart.

Hannah felt so grateful. All she needed was the love and support of Virginia. With a smile on her face, she took a piece of cake and savored the sweetness of both the dessert and the moment. She knew the road ahead would be full of challenges and trials, as it always had been for her, but for now, she was content to enjoy the warmth of the love and affection that surrounded her.

Virginia looked out the window. "It will be dark very soon, so I'm afraid it's too late to show you around today. I would have liked to show you a bit of the area before the sun goes down, as they've promised snow tomorrow, and I usually stay inside and work then."

Hannah suddenly realized that she didn't know what kind of job Virginia had. In fact, she knew nothing about her. She corrected herself, because there was ONE thing she did know with complete and utter certainty—and that was that Virginia was GOOD. There was no evil in her, and Virginia meant it when she said that she would always make sure that people around her felt good.

"Everything in this place whispers welcome home," said Virginia, who had obviously understood what Hannah's brain was tumbling over. "It's a place that connects to the heart, body, and soul. There are beautiful sunsets, lovely areas for long walks, ocean swimming when the weather is right. And maybe most importantly for you, it's also a place for new beginnings."

Hannah nodded, fascinated.

Virginia continued, "Plus, it's one of the few places here on the Danish West Coast where it's not that windy, so a lot of trees are able to grow. In fact, the trees were one of the things I fell in love with most. And then the wonderful, peaceful atmosphere, the unspoiled beach, and the incredibly varied landscape. There aren't many places in Denmark where you can find so many different types of landscape all in one place. The farm itself also appealed to me. It's full of history." Virginia pointed up at a sizable ornate beam in the ceiling. "That beam dates back to when the house was built. There are dates carved into it. At one point, it was infested with wood-boring beetles, but luckily, I got rid of them. So now it's treated and should last many years."

"Wood-boring beetles." Hannah gently touched the old beams. "I read about them in an old book. But I never dreamed I'd get to see where they lived."

Virginia smiled and took a hairpin out of her pinned-up hair, straightening it a bit before reattaching it—a habit she seemed to have. "Today, we'll have to settle for the main house. But tomorrow, when you're fresh and rested, I'll take you on a guided tour to see the whole farm, assuming the snow allows us."

"The Farm on The Edge of The World," Hannah murmured, entranced, looking out of the small old windows at the setting sun. The golden ball began to disappear into the North Sea. From where she stood, Hannah couldn't see the beach or the water's edge itself, but she could see water and the horizon as far as her eyes could wander. She walked to the window on the opposite side, viewing the courtyard. There stood an extensive collection of garden pots of all sizes and colors. As an artist, she immediately thought they would make the subject of a beautiful painting.

Virginia followed Hannah's gaze. "At this time of year, all the pots are empty, but you just wait until spring comes, and we'll fill them with flowers of every color. They always attract the most beautiful butterflies."

Hannah nodded and glanced up at the roof. The canopy looked disheveled, and mossy growths were growing on one side. "I've never seen a thatched roof in real life, only described in my books." Hannah suddenly thought of something else. "I've never swum in the sea either. I'm not really much of a swimmer though." She looked apologetically at Virginia, who had sat down in a rocking chair and was rocking softly.

"No, that's probably not what you did most back home in Copenhagen. But we'll soon teach you. It's not quite safe to bathe here, though. Calm water can hide great dangers. You must learn the signs of nature to feel safe on land and water."

Hannah nodded. "I will look forward to that. It's so beautiful here, and the sea looks so inviting."

"Out here on the North Sea, there are often big waves. They can seem quite violent, so people regularly head for areas of calm bathing water. But that's completely wrong." Virginia stopped the rocking chair and bent down, picking up a stray hairpin. "Lack of foam on the waves is often a sign that a hole has appeared in the sandbar right at that spot. And then, quite naturally, a powerful local current is generated away from the beach." She routinely twisted her hair into a soft bun and secured it with the newfound hairpin. "But don't worry; I'll take you for a swim when spring comes. For now, you'll just have to enjoy the view from the shore."

Hannah looked again at the thatched roof. She noticed that there were several places where birds had built nests. "It looks old." She looked questioningly at Virginia.

"It doesn't matter much to me what things look like. I actually like the roof the way it is now. But yes, you're right; it does need replacing. I'll have to make an appointment with a roofer when the weather warms up. It's no good having it start raining down in the light barn."

"Light barn? I've never heard of such a thing. What is a light barn?"

"I'll show you tomorrow. Now it's time to taste your birthday cake." Virginia found a small bag of tiny candles in a drawer and carefully placed eighteen of them in the birthday cake. "Happy birthday, my sweet girl!" Virginia arranged the whipped cream on top of the birthday cake. Hannah sat with tears in her eyes, looking at the flickering candles. "You don't know how grateful and happy I am that you took the time to do this for me." Hannah hugged the little woman in her arms. "I've never had a birthday cake with candles on my birthday."

She could still remember when she turned ten. She had been looking forward to it for weeks, imagining all the presents and surprises that awaited her. She had heard her mother talking in the bedroom. She hadn't been able to hear all the words, but it was something about a birthday and a big surprise. And turning ten was something special, so she had been sure that her mother had planned a surprise for her. But when the day arrived, it turned out to be nothing like what she had expected.

Her mother had clearly forgotten all about her birthday. There were no balloons, no decorations, no cake. Hannah tried not to show her disappointment, but her mother's indifference hurt her deeply.

"Didn't you buy me any presents?" she asked, trying to sound hopeful.

Her mother looked up from the perfumed letter she was reading. "There's money in the drawer, you can just buy anything you want."

Hannah's heart sank. Money was not what she wanted. She wanted her mother to remember her special day, to make her feel loved and appreciated. She wanted to feel like she mattered. Hannah shook off the thought of her tenth birthday and looked gratefully at Virginia.

"I am very, very grateful," Hannah repeated, smiling warmly at Virginia.

"That's good, my sweet girl, because the moment you express gratitude, you'll find your focus shifts immediately. You will begin to attract better and more positive things. After all, it's impossible to go back and change the beginning. The time that has passed cannot be altered. But you can begin to change the life you want to live in the future. From the moment you get the idea that there is something you want to change, you can start doing it."

"How do I know what needs to change?" Hannah was ready to do whatever Virginia wanted her to do. "Is it something about clairvoyance? Or palm reading?"

"No, my sweet girl." Virginia's voice was steadfast. "At my house, we always use our heads. Everything I do is guided by my common sense. My dress style may indicate otherwise, but I take responsibility for my life and do so with reason and logic as my main tools. Everything you need to know is in your head. You just need to learn how to use it correctly, and that's what I can help you with. I can do that because I've studied and read extensively about using our common sense as a guideline through life. I've also practiced it for many years, and have much experience to put in."

"It sounds fascinating. Please tell me more. I want to study and get to know everything you do."

Virginia interrupted her. "Later, my girl. I want to hear about your trip to New York and why you're already home. But first, you must sleep."

Chapter 10

A beautiful and quiet tributary appeared, tempting for a little detour. But the tributary quickly changed character from quiet, beautiful, and calm to wild and violent, with several smaller rapids and a single waterfall.

The next morning, just after eating a delicious breakfast of freshly baked muffins and homemade jam, Virginia settled into the rocking chair. "Now, I'm ready to hear about your exciting trip to the city that never sleeps." She let out a little fart and set the rocking chair in motion. "Tell me everything and from the beginning! You know I want to hear it all. Even the things you'd rather forget."

～

Hannah started telling, sighed, and re-experienced the pain she'd felt on the plane to New York.

A small, thin woman who was sitting on the seat by the window looked sourly at her, making an effort to fill as much of the narrow airplane seat as possible. "People with legs that long should stand up so there can be room for us regular people too!" "Sorry." Hannah pressed herself closer together in the seat next to the thin lady, not quite understanding what she meant. After all, you weren't allowed to stand up on the plane. Hannah tried to pull her legs together, but it was simply impossible. Suddenly she felt a finger poking her in the stomach and reluctantly turned toward the person sitting on the seat by the aisle.

"Feel free to lean against me." The man who had poked her in the stomach smiled at her. "I have a soft shoulder you can rest your head on, and you can also rest your long legs over mine."

He tried to catch her eye, but Hannah bowed her head and mumbled, "No thanks." She just wanted to be left alone and try to sort out her heavy thoughts.

She had been at her father's office to pick up her belongings. They could easily fit in two suitcases and a backpack. The journey from the office to the airport and onto the plane was in a gray haze. But this began an entirely new chapter in her life. She was on her way to New York. To a big city where no one knew her—a city where she could easily disappear into the crowd.

The annoying man beside her poked at her again. *What was wrong with him?* She spent nine very uncomfortable hours with the angry lady on one side and the pushy man on the other before the plane finally touched the ground.

Hannah picked up her backpack and looked stiffly ahead, pretending not to notice several people looking at her curiously.

A few comments reached her.

"Giraffe girl," "Avatar," "Skyscraper..."

She bowed her head even more and walked purposefully toward the baggage claim to get her suitcases, and then outside to the waiting taxis.

"Is this your first visit to New York?" The cab driver, a young Black man with a broad smile, chatted politely, but Hannah was engrossed in her own wistful thoughts and didn't answer. She was already beginning to regret not having stayed in Denmark. If she had stayed then perhaps she would have been able to continue her conversations with Virginia.

Hannah's lack of interest proved of no consequence, however, for the young driver chatted away, pointing and telling:

"My name is Joe. This job as a taxi driver is my first real job," Joe smiled proudly. "I'm going to make a lot of money. Just look at all those people who need to be driven somewhere. It's going to be great." He glanced happily at Hannah and pointed out things he thought would interest her whenever they drove by.

Only when absolutely necessary did Hannah answer him with monosyllables. Thoughts about her past and, above all, the fear of the unknown future that lay ahead of her swirled in her poor head, but she kept coming to the same conclusion. She couldn't have done anything but say yes to the trip to New York her father had set in motion. She saw nothing and felt nothing. Everything was gray, and as always, when there was something she couldn't handle, she kept it all trapped inside. Was it perhaps herself she was running away from?

Joe stopped the car at the art school. He opened his door and walked around to the trunk, where he lifted her suitcases out. "If you need a cab, feel free to call me." He handed Hannah a crumpled card as she got out of the car.

Hannah automatically tucked the card into the pocket of her jeans and, as she often did before, grabbed the hairpin Virginia had forgotten the last time she visited Hannah in the hospital. Hannah touched the hairpin several times a day and felt how the touch relaxed her each time.

Hannah looked at the big old house with its weathered brick walls and white-framed windows that would be her home for the next six months. She stopped for a moment in front of the wide staircase leading up to the front door. On the bottom step stood a colossal sculpture depicting an imaginatively made dragon, spreading its wings so that one might risk falling over them if not careful.

One, two, three, ten steps up. Hannah hesitated in front of the door and turned to look down the street. The street was lined with trees on both sides, their leaves swaying gently in the breeze and casting shadows on the sidewalk below. There were very few parked cars and several of the houses on the street had front gardens with well-tended small lawns. The people walking by seemed to have plenty of time. She was aware she was stalling as she let her eyes slide down the beautiful wrought iron banister instead of knocking on the door.

A yellow cab stopped, and a young guy jumped out and handed a pile of cash to the driver. He was not quite as tall as her and was wearing jeans and carrying a sketchbook. His hair was long and flopped around his ears. The young guy looked up and smiled broadly when he spotted Hannah at the door. "Hey there." He took the stairs in three jumps. "I'm Simon." He hesitated for a fraction of a second before setting his bags down and giving her a huge hug.

Hannah stiffened. Who was he? She did not come to New York to find a new boyfriend. She was done with that. Never again. That was for sure. She didn't like his scrutinizing look. It was as if he was trying to undress her with his eyes to use her body in a painting.

"What's the name of this hot chick standing in front of me?"

"Hannah." She turned toward the door and used the heavy knocker hanging in the middle of it. She hoped someone would come out so she could escape this strange guy.

A burly middle-aged woman wearing a paint-stained jumpsuit opened the door and showed them both into the foyer, looking curiously at Hannah. "You must be the Danish girl. My old friend, John's daughter."

Hannah nodded but didn't answer.

"You are tall. I don't think I've ever seen such a tall girl before. It's strange. You must be taller than your father."

Hannah sighed inwardly. Had her father been fooling around with ladies over here too? Yes, of course, he had. Hannah took a firm grip on her suitcases and followed the woman who was already halfway up the stairs to the first floor.

The woman kept talking as she walked up the stairs. "The boys live on the first floor and the girls on the fourth. And the boys are not allowed to go to the fourth floor." She gave Simon a firm look and quickly showed him to a room on the first floor before continuing up the stairs with Hannah. "The second and third floors are devoted to the arts and workshops and the top floor is where all you girls stay." She stopped in front of a door on the right and opened it.

"Here's your room," she said, stepping aside so Hannah could peek in.

Hannah stared in amazement at the four narrow beds. The room was large and bright, and next to each bed was a large chest of drawers. In the center of the room was a round table with four easels around it. The walls were bare, but nail marks showed that there used to be pictures hanging there. "Don't I get my own room?" She had trouble expressing herself in English, which sounded slightly stuttering, but the lady apparently understood her well.

"You'll be staying in a four-bed room, but you're lucky because only two other girls are coming this semester. One of the girls apparently had a last-minute change of heart. But you'd better get unpacked. I'll meet you in the dining room in half an hour. I'm Jane, by the way." The lady disappeared out the door, leaving a disoriented Hannah alone in the room.

꩜

The first week had passed relatively well, but Hannah had an uncomfortable feeling of being really small (an odd feeling for her) and unable to fend for herself in the big city. The buildings were enormous, the sounds loud, and the smells constantly changed from burnt fuel to garbage odors to delicious and savory from the many food trucks and street vendors.

Hannah stopped in front of one of the classic old fire escapes. The fire escapes added an extra layer of texture to the buildings, giving them a rugged, industrial feel. And they appeared to be both functional and decorative, with their curving shapes and ornate metalwork, and normally Hannah would have loved to explore all the details, but she felt completely worn out. New York looked exactly like what she had often seen in movies and read about, yet it was different. It was real, but it felt more like she was in a bad movie, and all she saw was empty scenery with no substance.

Hannah's brain was tired and couldn't take in all the impressions. Everything was mixed up—good style, bad style, poor, rich—everything placed right on top of each other. It was all just too much. She felt the city was dirty, strange, messy, and chaotic. There was dull gray concrete everywhere, interspersed with broken railroad tracks. She didn't register that it was also beautiful and charming, and that people smiled when they walked down the street. It didn't register that others could be happy. That was not an emotion with which she was very familiar. Hannah was in a state of hopelessness and saw only the negative.

On her long legs, she walked almost every day. And when she went for a walk, she was safe from Simon's unpleasant attempts to grope her. He had already managed more than once to sneak up on her from behind and grab her breasts. She walked from Midtown down to Greenwich Village and Soho, and from there to Chinatown. She saw all the sights and the view of the famous skyline in the background, but she saw it all through a haze of hopelessness. She walked across the Brooklyn Bridge, through Wall Street, and down to the waterfront. There, she watched the Statue of Liberty in the background before sighing deeply, turning around, and walking back the exact same way. New city, but same walking around looking for something … anything. She tried to find a regular route like the one she had so often walked in Copenhagen, but it was all too confusing for her.

Back home in Copenhagen, she loved walking around the city and feeling like she was part of life, even if she wasn't actively participating. In New York, she felt totally out of place. Suddenly, the loneliness crept in—the sad loneliness one can feel when they are among many people. Hannah felt the tears pressing on and stopped and rummaged in her bag for a Kleenex.

At that moment, it started to rain. Big heavy drops hit the back of Hannah's neck. She looked up with a sigh. Her attire today was definitely not suitable for rainy weather of that caliber. She had been so absorbed in gloomy thoughts that she hadn't even noticed the sky had morphed into something dark and threatening. She sighed again, and at once, it began to thunder violently. It was certainly no tiny shower. The raindrops were icy cold, hitting her nylon stocking-clad legs like a shower of pebbles. She crossed the street, hoping to find some shelter along the tall building opposite, but the wind whipped the rain almost horizontally against the building, so it didn't help. She spotted a sign.

Ristorante Ernesto - Sardinian Specialties. It would be nice to try something new. She liked Italian food. In the past, she had often borrowed books from the library about Italian cooking, so she knew a little about the cuisine. She was struck by the warm and cozy atmosphere, with dim lighting and rustic decor. There were woven baskets hanging from the ceiling, and colorful fabrics draped over the chairs and tables. And some Italian music was playing softly in the background. More than half of the twenty or so tables were occupied and Hannah quickly looked around and chose the most secluded table, right by the kitchen.

Hannah looked at the menu that was chalked on a large black board on the end wall. There were several dishes she didn't even know existed. She read, *Culurgiones d'Ogliastra*. It sounded exciting. Hannah wondered if the waiter understood English and could explain the dish.

The elderly waiter smiled and explained in broken English. "It's a special Sardinian ravioli filled with ricotta, spinach, and saffron. The ravioli is covered with a rich and flavorful tomato sauce just before serving and sprinkled with freshly grated pecorino."

Ravioli! Finally, something she knew. She nodded to the waiter and looked around the restaurant. It was cozy and rustic, and the scent of fresh food being prepared and cooked from the kitchen made her mouth water.

A middle-aged woman with a haunted look brought Hannah her soft drink and left immediately.

Something was going on in the kitchen, though. There were several loud noises, and when Hannah turned, startled, an elderly waiter rushed out with a plate of pasta. Another loud noise made him flinch and drop the plate on Hannah's right shoulder, sending thick red pasta sauce down her dress and into her lap.

"Your dress! It's ruined!" The middle-aged woman came running with a stack of napkins and began to wipe her off.

There was another noise from the kitchen, and this time, a short, chubby man with a very tall chef's hat came running toward the waiter waving a wet dish towel. He began to hit the man with loud slaps.

Hannah sat silent with her head bowed, wondering what on earth was going on, wishing she were anywhere but in a restaurant populated by unpleasant and erratic people. It was a pity because the food smelled so delicious. She thoughtfully dipped a finger into the thick red pasta sauce in her lap and tasted it. Uhm ... really superb. She was about to repeat the process when the angry chef spotted her and came at her at high speed.

"Who do you think you are? You just scared my waiter so much that he dropped my amazing food. Do you have any idea how many hours I spent in the kitchen making that pasta?"

Startled, she let out a very loud fart. "Sorry, I didn't mean to..." Hannah was so embarrassed, she wished she could have melted right into the floor beneath her.

"What the hell do you think you're doing? Are you sitting in my restaurant taking a shit? While other people are eating lunch?"

The middle-aged woman, who was about to start wiping Hannah's dress, left the napkins and fled. The angry cook approached, and Hannah, looking at him in fright, quickly got up from her chair, hoping to escape to the street, away from the furious man.

The cook positioned himself right behind her, grabbed the damp dish towel, and began hitting Hannah's bottom.

Suddenly everything turned into a farce. The few other diners in the restaurant stretched their necks to watch the scene, but none of them did anything to stop the furious man with the wet towel.

The furious man looked down at the floor beneath Hannah's chair. There was a large wet spot on the floor where she had been sitting. "What the hell. Did you piss on my floor too?"

"It's just rainwater." Hannah tried to explain, but when the cook once again hit her on the butt, this time quite hard, she decided that it was better to get away in a hurry before things got worse.

Hannah put one long leg in front of the other and reached the door. She looked back fearfully, and the last thing she heard the angry cook shout before the door closed behind her was, "*Dio Santo!*" And then she saw another slap as the angry chef hit the old waiter with the wet towel.

Hannah headed straight for the nearest taxi and almost fell into the back seat. She straightened her wet dress soaked in red sauce and rainwater and got some grease on her hand, and a small smile spread across her face. A ravioli had been hiding in her pocket. Should she eat it? After what she just went through, she thought why not? She felt a firework of wonderful flavors explode in her mouth and sighed distractedly. It was almost worth going back there again sometime just to eat that crazy chef's food.

After a few weeks, things got a little better. Hannah smiled to herself and thought about how quickly she got used to sharing a room with two other girls! Laura and Nicole were kind to her, and Laura, in particular, was very sweet and easy to talk to. Laura, who had grown up in Boston, was a warm and compassionate girl, with a naturally kind and gentle demeanor. She was always quick with a smile or a kind word and Hannah admired her beautiful blonde hair and the calm confidence she exuded. She felt that some of that confidence transferred to herself.

The black-haired Nicole with the short hair was a few years older than Laura and herself, and she was a little harder to figure out. There was something about her that could be a little scary at times, even if it was never directly expressed in her behavior. But she was kind and she had a funny sense of humor and could make Hannah laugh without her being able to say afterwards what it was that had been so funny.

Right now, Laura was busy fixing Hannah up.

"It's my birthday present to you now that you've turned eighteen. But don't look in the mirror yet. Wait until I'm completely done with your makeup and hair." Laura gently brushed Hannah's soft dark hair with the golden streaks and parted it with the curling iron on one side, twisting a soft curl around her finger. She continued purposefully, curling, twisting, and squeezing waves into her hair right down at the scalp, making Hannah's hair appear even more extensive and voluminous, curling beautifully down, framing her neck in a way that highlighted her pronounced cheekbones. "Turn around and tell me what you think!" Laura had an infectious grin, and her light blue eyes played in the small piquant face framed by blonde hair.

"You've done something to make me look at least ten years older and much more sophisticated." Hannah viewed her new look from all angles. "It's a lovely birthday present. I am very grateful that you take the time to do all this for someone like me." She stretched to her full height.

Laura laughed. "The two of us together look so funny." She shook her long blonde hair. "I can just reach your chin when I'm on my toes!"

Hannah watched her friend through half-closed eyes. It was strange, but it only took a few weeks before she felt really comfortable with Laura. There was something about her that made Hannah feel safe and secure. It had been like that almost from the start, and she grew to like her more and more every day. It was an indescribably wonderful feeling to finally have a friend. Hannah gave her a warm smile. "We are very different, but that's probably why we get along so well. I don't have any need to put on makeup and curl my hair on a daily basis. But if someday I feel like I've accomplished something great myself, and therefore deserve something extra, I'll either do my hair exactly this way or, better yet, have you do it for me again. Is that a deal?" Hannah blew a small fart, and Laura grinned and demonstratively covered her nose.

"Yes, of course, but we'd better finish our homework. We have an art history test tomorrow. I want a good result to impress my dad."

Hannah looked enviously at Laura. "Your father cares about you, doesn't he?"

Laura nodded and looked at Hannah, puzzled.

"What does your father do for a living?"

"He runs the family business. It's nothing exciting, just something with books." Laura threw herself onto the bed and Hannah threw herself down next to her and tried to give her friend a loving hug, something she had never done before.

"Don't touch me. Don't ever touch me." Laura jumped from the bed with a look on her face that Hannah had never seen before. An expression of fear and disgust.

"I'm sorry, I just..."

"Don't ever touch me; I hate it when people touch me." Laura walked out of the room and slammed the door.

Hannah was left with a strange feeling that something was very wrong, and from that day on, there was an inexplicable change in their relationship. Laura was still kind and they could laugh and have fun, but Laura kept Hannah at a distance in a way that puzzled and surprised her. But she made no attempt to find out what was wrong. She never asked what the problem was. As always, she automatically assumed that it was her fault. She assumed that Laura no longer felt safe and secure when she was with her.

And a couple of days later, when Hannah came into the room after once again pushing Simon away when he tried to grab her bottom, she found Nicole alone in the room and Laura's part of the room completely empty of belongings.

"Where is Laura? Has she moved to another room?" Hannah looked from the empty bed and back to Nicole, who was standing against the wall. "Do you know what happened?"

"Some money is missing," Nicole replied.

"Money? What do you mean? What money?" Hannah understood less and less of what was going on.

Nicole came closer and let her gaze drift over Hannah's tall body. "Several of the other girls have complained to Jane that their money is missing."

"But what does this have to do with Laura?"

"Laura recently told me that her father's business wasn't doing so well. That he was afraid of going bankrupt. Maybe she needed some money..." Nicole didn't finish the sentence, but looked at Hannah to see if she understood what she meant.

"You mean Laura stole money?" Hannah asked in disbelief.

"I'm just telling you what people are talking about," Nicole shrugged. "But it might be wise to check that your money is where it should be."

Hannah checked her backpack. All her cash was gone. She turned to Nicole in panic. "Why would Laura do such a thing? What the hell am I supposed to do now?"

"I have money," Nicole reassured her. "You don't have to worry about money. I have plenty for both of us."

Hannah was lost in thought, not hearing what Nicole was saying. Everyone she cared about disappeared from her life. She turned to Nicole. "It's weird Laura didn't say goodbye..."

"Never mind, we don't want to think about that anymore," Nicole changed the subject. "What do you have against men, anyway?"

"Nothing. I don't understand."

"Remember those times when we talked about our crushes?"

Hannah nodded, thinking back to the very few details she had shared with the other two girls. She had only told them that she had lived with Anders for a couple of years and that he had been mean to her when he had been drinking and had died in an accident just before she came to New York. She hadn't told them anything about the child she had lost, nor any details about the many humiliations that Anders inflicted on her. After all, it was all her fault. Deep in her heart, she knew it was an illogical thought, but it would never leave her. She was the cause of all the misfortunes. It had always been that way and she feared it would always remain that way.

Nicole looked at her with a strange look in her eyes. "You're acting like a woman who's been deeply hurt."

Hannah avoided meeting Nicole's gaze. "I have no idea what you're talking about."

"Nonsense," Nicole said firmly. "You just don't want to talk about it, but you need to move on and get it out of your system."

Hannah scowled at her friend. "Do you realize what Anders did to me? How the hell am I supposed to forgive him?"

Nicole shook her head. "I don't know what he did, and I didn't mean for you to forgive him. But I know what you can do to forget him."

"Will you tell me how?" Hannah asked eagerly. She wanted nothing more than to forget about her painful past with Anders.

Nicole sat down on the bed and patted the seat next to her. "Sit next to me, and I'll tell you MY story."

Hannah sat on the edge of the bed, sensing something in the air that she couldn't place. Nicole abruptly changed the subject once more. "You love to draw, don't you?"

"Well, we all do here. That's why we're in art class," Hannah replied, confused.

"Then draw me naked!" Nicole rose from the bed and stripped down so quickly that Hannah didn't have time to react. Nicole posed provocatively, revealing her slim, boyish body.

"What the hell are you doing?" Hannah jumped off the bed, trying to get past her naked friend.

"Look, I'm completely flat here just like a boy," Nicole said, pressing her hands against her chest. "I'll never hurt you. I'll be nice to you. I love you, love you dearly in all the ways that love can be expressed."

"NO!" Hannah pushed her away.

"You just have to let me love you. It will be so good for both of us. I know it will. You're my best friend. My only friend." Nicole became hysterical, and Hannah felt like she was falling into a bottomless abyss.

"Well, you're my best friend too," Hannah said, pulling back a little so that her back was against the easel. If Laura had still been there, she wouldn't have said that.

"You said you like the way I look."

"I do. It suits you perfectly."

Nicole fell to her knees.

"Oh no, you don't mean that. You simply can't mean that." Hannah observed the naked body before her and understood that Nicole meant every word. "I'm sorry." Hannah moved herself back towards the door, with Nicole clinging to her arm. "But I don't love you like that."

"Have you ever made love to a woman?"

"No."

"Then you don't know. Because we are women, we can love each other fully and be each other's soulmates."

Hannah shook her head and tore herself away. "No, it's not like that. I KNOW that. I'm not sexually attracted to you, even though I love you in a friendship kind of way."

"You can be attracted to me if you just let me love you."

"I can't, and I won't. It's not right for me. I just know that. It has nothing to do with you; it's just me being that way."

"Will you give us a chance later? Will you let me make love to you and show you how amazing it can be?"

"I can't." Hannah found an unknown inner strength. She wasn't used to saying no but knew she had to stand firm on her decision this time.

"Having sex with you would be wonderful." Nicole moved close to Hannah and tiptoed, trying to kiss her mouth. "Let's make love now, and we'll have everything together. We could leave school and move in together for real. Now that you're eighteen, you can decide for yourself. I have enough money so we can rent a small apartment and be together all the time."

Hannah stepped backward and protectively held out her arms to keep Nicole at bay.

"You have to stop this right now! It will never happen! I can't love you your way, only my own."

Nicole suddenly sent her a look so filled with hate that Hannah flinched. "I hate you! I'm destroying you! If you don't make love to me today, I'll fucking destroy you!"

Hannah looked at Nicole with tears in her eyes. "You have to do what you feel is right for you, just like I do what I feel is right for

ME." With these words, Hannah walked out the door, leaving the naked Nicole all alone in the room.

※

Hannah was sitting on the bottom step of the stairs with her arms around the dragon sculpture when Simon walked by. He looked curiously at her, as it was obvious that she had been crying.

"Why are you sitting here?"

"I have no money," cried Hannah and banged her forehead against the dragon figure in an attempt to replace the pain inside her with an external pain. "All my money's gone. Someone has stolen it."

"Why do you need money?" Simon sat down next to her.

"I want to go home—home to Denmark. I can't stay here anymore."

Simon looked at her thoughtfully. "If you're willing to pay the price, I'll give you money for the plane ticket and a little extra for the trip."

Hannah gave an almost silent little fart. "What price?"

"I want a whole night with you." He looked her straight in the eyes.

"A whole night." Hannah hesitated. "You mean sex?"

"Yes, of course. I want to spend a whole night having sex with you. I'll give you all the money you need if you give me sex. I have enough money, as you know. My old man is filthy rich."

Hannah looked him straight in the eye. "I'm NOT into hardcore sex, but if you agree to be gentle with me, I will do it." She cringed inside as she thought back to her time with Anders. It was just something that needed to be done as quickly as possible. At the time, she didn't even think about the fact that it made a big difference whether one had sex because they wanted to or whether one did it for money.

He nodded. "That's okay."

"And I have one more condition. We will stay at a hotel where no one knows us."

"Deal!" Simon took her hand. "Just pack your stuff, I'll get a cab, and we'll get going. I know a quiet hotel where we can stay." Simon didn't mention that he had been there several times when he needed a woman, and he could always find a willing woman who bit the hook.

Hannah immediately went to her room and packed up her things, two suitcases and a backpack. Exactly the same things she had brought with her when she arrived a few weeks ago. None of the pictures she had painted in the weeks she had been in New York were going home with her. They were ugly and gloomy and all she wanted to do was forget about them. She suddenly thought of something and quickly scribbled a few words on a piece of paper and threw it on her bed. It was no good if they thought she had disappeared. She took one last look around the room with the four beds before she sighed deeply and started dragging her belongings down the stairs. She continued out the front door without saying goodbye to a single person.

As promised, Simon had already arranged for a taxi to wait for them at the curb.

Hannah unwound her long body from the taxi and looked at the hotel. It was a cheap, cozy art-deco place in the middle of Midtown. It was obviously a building that had once been grand and luxurious, but now showed all the signs of neglect and decay.

It was adorned with intriguing geometric patterns, but the paint was peeling or faded. Puzzled, Hannah stepped into the lobby with

Simon's arm firmly around her back, as if he was afraid she would change her mind and disappear before he got what he wanted.

The polished marble floors in the lobby were cracked and stained and the middle-aged man at the reception desk was surrounded by stacks of dusty papers.

Simon said something to the man that Hannah didn't catch, but suddenly he was holding a large heavy key and leading her up a narrow staircase to the first floor. She didn't know what to expect, but considering Simon always bragged about his money, she'd expected a hotel of a slightly higher standard.

The room was on the first floor, with a window opening onto a half-meter-wide back alley where virtually no light could enter. A room in which you had no idea whether it was night or day.

It was dark and gloomy, and Hannah felt an intangible terror. What on earth had she said yes to?

Simon locked the door behind them and pulled off his T-shirt. He grinned at her and stepped out of his jeans. He wasn't wearing boxers, and there was no doubt he was more than ready for sex.

Suddenly, he startled Hannah. It was the first time since she had been living with Anders that she was with a man who was expecting sex. Sure, Simon had promised that he wouldn't do anything that caused her pain, but could she trust him? She felt a wild urge to jump up and run away. He grinned at her. "What you see is what you get."

She had to go through with it. She simply had to get home. Home? Why did she say that? She didn't have a home.

Simon reached out and pulled her against his powerful erection. "Are you ready for me?" He pulled up her dress and rubbed it against her pussy.

Hannah was standing as stiff as a board.

"You're not a virgin, are you?" Simon released her and looked at her in wonder.

"No," she shook her head and began to unbutton her dress in slow motion.

"Nice tits you have. Take off your bra so I can get a better look at them."

"No." She closed her eyes. Simon could do what he wanted with her, but she wouldn't actively participate.

His arms closed around her, and he unclasped her bra. "Lovely tits." He bit one nipple, ripped off her panties, and penetrated her without more foreplay.

Hannah lay completely apathetic and let Simon do what he wanted.

After a few minutes, he collapsed on top of her. "You don't say a fucking thing, and you just lie there playing starfish. A dead starfish. That's the worst sex I've ever had. If you want my money, you'd better start acting as if you like it. I'm going to get some sleep, and then you can give me a blowjob."

Hannah sighed inwardly. She didn't like doing it, but she had done it on Anders many times before, and she knew she had the technique in place. She turned her back to Simon and lay perfectly still, hoping it would be a long time before he woke up.

Her prayers went unanswered, for not even half an hour had passed before Simon lay down on his back.

"Now, you must show me what you can do for me. I've brought the money and will only pay for complete satisfaction!"

/2

Simon's parting words, as he handed her the promised money, said it all.

"You're fucking good at blowjobs. You could easily make a lot of money doing it, and you've already done it for money. Once a whore, always a whore!"

"Are you feeling unwell?" The kind lady at the hotel reception looked at Hannah as she descended after pleasing Simon not once, but three times.

The lady stopped Hannah as she was about to step onto the street. "You look like you should have stayed in bed."

Hannah shook her head. "No, I'm not sick."

"Have you been out partying all night, perhaps?"

"No, I never go out at night." She had spent the whole night in bed with a man she did not love, a man she did not even like. A man who had paid her money for it! She felt disgusting and dirty.

"I thought so. It must be a man—I've seen it before." The lady pointed to a soft chair in the far corner. "Sit there, and I'll bring you a nice cup of hot chocolate. You need it." The woman went to a coffee machine and pressed a few buttons.

"Thank you." Hannah drifted over to the chair and gratefully accepted the hot chocolate, carefully drinking from the warm mug. She instinctively stuck her hand in her pocket to touch Virginia's old, worn hairpin.

Hannah rose with a start and felt the world collapse around her. The hairpin was gone! She frantically rummaged in her pocket again and pulled out a crumpled card. She groaned and looked at the card. Was it a sign?

She took out her phone and dialed the number on the card.

"I hope you haven't been waiting too long. I came as soon as I could." Joe opened the trunk and put her suitcases and her backpack inside. "Where do you want to be driven today?" He looked at her curiously. She had looked tired and lethargic when he had driven her from the airport a few weeks ago, but now she looked like she could barely stay upright.

"To the airport, please." Hannah folded her legs, slid into the back seat, sighed, and looked out the window at the beautiful skyline on the horizon. It was a pity that she had not made the most of her exciting stay in New York. There were so many beautiful and exciting places she should have visited. But she hadn't been up to it.

Hannah bowed her head and fell into deep thought. Deep down, she knew in a strange, subconscious way that one day she would return to the city that never sleeps, and then she would be ready.

Chapter 11

Back in the mother river, the great sandbar of the finest white sand was visible on the horizon again. The current was steady, and the pace was pleasant.

Hannah sighed and took Virginia's hand. "I didn't feel comfortable in New York at all. There were so many people. Sometimes I felt like New York was one big nightmare after another."

Virginia smiled at her. "There are eight million people in New York City alone, my sweet girl. All crammed into an area the size of Bornholm, so you can't choose who you want to see. Rich, poor, homeless, famous, nice, stupid, crazy—all melted into one big pot."

"Have you ever been to New York?" Hannah asked, surprised.

"Yes," Virginia nodded, "when I was young." She didn't elaborate but threw a whisk to Hannah and continued, "Will you be so kind as to whisk the eggs?" Virginia fetched the fresh seaweed and began to rinse it.

Hannah took the whisk but stayed with it in her hand, looking at Virginia. "Now you know everything. You know I went to New York as a nice girl and came home a whore. That I had sex for money. I ruined Laura's and Nicole's lives because of who I am. Because I always cause pain wherever I go."

"That's bullshit." Virginia let the seaweed be and gave Hannah a big hug. "It's not your fault that others behave weirdly or rudely.

You can never be responsible for what others say, think, or do." Virginia gently released her and asked a question. "Do you think Laura took your money?"

"I don't know. I thought she was nice, and I don't want to believe that about her, but the money was gone, and Laura disappeared simultaneously. So, what else should I think?"

Virginia didn't answer the question but said, "Every time you take something from someone, you lose something of yourself, and every time you give something to someone, you get a lot more back. You must always remember to give."

Hannah looked at her in amazement. "But I have nothing to give."

"That's not true; you have a thousand things you can give to others that they will be grateful for."

"But I don't have any money or valuables—no jewelry or anything." Her voice became high and self-righteous. "That's why I had to have sex with Simon."

Virginia ignored her outburst and continued, "Stealing is never the way to get anything. Instead, ask yourself, what can I do for them? Is there anything I'm so good at that other people will pay me to do it?"

Hannah stood silently, still with the whisk in her hand, not knowing what to say.

"Everyone has something they're good at, something they can give. Give either to make money or just because it's nice to give. If you give without expecting anything in return, you'll find that other people start giving to you too."

Hannah sighed and said, "I get the point, but I'm not sure what I'm good at."

"That's all right, my sweet girl. Let's talk about it some other time. And as for your trip to New York, I must admit, I was expecting something like that. Well, not exactly the Nicole and Simon things, but I didn't expect that you would have the good experience you hoped for."

Hannah looked at Virginia's gentle face, surprised. "What do you mean?"

"You weren't looking forward to an exciting trip. You were looking for an escape. But you weren't mentally ready for the big change, and that's completely understandable. But let's leave all that behind us and look ahead. Now let me ask you—what would you like to do now?"

Hannah didn't hesitate. "I want to stay here with you."

Virginia patted her cheek. "I'm very pleased about that. I already care for you deeply and would love to be the one to show you the way—the right way, the way you must take to fulfill your dreams and reach your goals."

"How do I know which way is right?" Hannah tried to hold back a fart, but it snuck between her buttocks.

"The wind and weather will have their way," Virginia replied with a grin. "Now remember, never hold back a fart—you'll get a stomachache. And what you don't have in your hands, you can't hold!"

Hannah giggled, and Virginia continued, "You have to learn to listen to yourself and your needs, and once you learn that you'll find the right path, YOUR way. But enough about that. The snow has stopped, and the sun is shining. The weather is lovely. A little cold, but what can you expect on a January day? It's time to show you around and take you to the edge of the world!"

Hannah looked at the roaring North Sea. "It makes me feel so small, but somehow safe too. Like no one will notice me here, like I can be exactly the person I want to be, and no one will raise an eyebrow at that."

"Yes, the ocean makes us feel small and insignificant. But only a fool does not fear the sea. It is so powerful that no human can control it."

Hannah let her eyes wander 360 degrees. There were marshes, dunes, hills, and a beautiful forest not too far from the flats, and in the middle of it all was the farm.

The Farm on The Edge of The World! It was almost right on the slope that led down to the beach.

"Do you own the farm?"

Virginia shook her head. "I don't own it, but I've rented it, and I'm allowed to live here as long as I live." There was something in Virginia's expression that kept Hannah from inquiring further.

Hannah thought of something else. "Don't you have a job?"

"Yes, my girl, I do work a lot, but I work here. I would not thrive at all with a nine to five office job. I need to be the boss of my own life. I decide how much I want to work and when."

"But what do you do for work?"

"I help people who are in need. There are always people who are perplexed and need my help. And they pay me to make use of my vast knowledge."

"How do these people find you here in the middle of nowhere?"

"They find me, or I find them. That's the way it has always been. Sometimes I'm swamped, and sometimes there's little to be done. But I don't need much. Nature gives a lot for free, as long as you know how to use it."

Virginia handed Hannah a wooden stick. "Here, you'll need this until you know the area better. In several places, you will have to cross a stream or a small ravine, and the stick will help. It will also be a good help when you go up and down the slope."

Hannah took the stick from Virginia's outreached hand and gently tapped it against the ground.

"There are a lot of dunes around here. They are formed by shifting sands, that is, by the movement of the wind." Virginia flapped her arms. "As you can see, many so-called pockets are in the sand. Smaller or larger pockets will protect you from the wind. And such a pocket can be used for other things, too." Virginia suddenly got a naughty look in her eyes. "Not so long ago I was laying in one of those pockets. We had a lot of fun." Virginia looked at Hannah to see if she got the hint, but Hannah was utterly engrossed in the landscape. "At first glance, the landscape seems monotonous, but when I look closer, there's a huge difference between how it looks when I'm standing down on the beach or farther back toward the forest."

"Yes, the western landscape here is a primeval wonder. Farther back toward the forest, you'll even find a couple of nice streams with fresh water too."

"Are there any dangerous animals here?" Hannah suddenly realized that her knowledge of wildlife could have been more extensive. Granted, she had always read a lot, but it was mostly about cities and people.

"All the smaller animals, like rabbits and foxes, are always here." Virginia scratched her hair, not noticing that two hairpins fell out, leaving her long hair blowing around her ears. She added, "There aren't many vipers here, so you'll be lucky if you see one. Vipers can feel the vibrations in the ground when we approach, and even though it's Denmark's only poisonous snake, it will always scurry away when we humans approach."

"I don't think I want to see a snake." Hannah pressed out a startled little fart, picked up the two hairpins, and put them in her pocket. "When's the best chance of seeing one?" She shuddered at the thought of being surprised by a poisonous snake.

"When it's cool in the morning, it typically moves sluggishly into the sun to warm up. So that's when you're most likely to see them." Virginia continued briskly up hills, down hills, over small ravines, and across a flat stretch of bristling marram grass. Hannah struggled to keep up, using her stick for help.

A loud chirp made Hannah look up as a large white and brown bird flew overhead, emitting one chirp after another.

"You can see a lot of different birds around here. It's a bird lover's paradise." Virginia, breathing effortlessly, looked at Hannah, who was tired, breathing heavy and strained. "The one you just saw was a greenshank."

"Which bird is your favorite?" Hannah paused and huffed.

"My favorite bird is the great copperhead. It can grow to be almost half a meter and has the most beautiful coppery colors and a very long pointed beak, so it can easily find food in shallow water."

"You know so much," Hannah sighed enviously.

"After all, I've lived out here for many years," Virginia added. "And right here on the world's edge, you might be lucky and spot a sea eagle." She ran off, leaping elegantly and gracefully, despite her short legs, over a small stream that curved through the landscape.

Hannah was suddenly embarrassed that her fatigue was so evident and used her stick as a makeshift pole vault across the stream. But she didn't jump far enough and ended up in cold water up to her knees. Virginia laughed and reached out her cane to Hannah to help her up.

A little farther on was a meadow where a snowstorm last week had left the grass patchy, covered with dirty gray snow. Hannah slipped on the icy ground and toppled over into a thorny thicket.

"Ouch!" Hannah looked at her hand, where a long thorn had attached itself.

Two pheasants exploded out of the thicket at once, first the hen, brown and dull, then the handsome male pheasant with scarlet cheeks and plumage that played in myriad beautiful colors. With the hen in the lead, the two birds rose ever higher into the air, and the wind caught them both and threw them higher above the treetops.

Hannah watched the beautiful sight, forgetting her wet feet and the thorn in her hand. "This is so beautiful... Beautiful and wild and yet peaceful."

"There are high ceilings out here," Virginia smiled, "room to think. To think big thoughts. But come, now it's time to show you the most important part of the farm. The long wing located right on the edge of the world."

Virginia trotted briskly up the steep wooden stairs from the beach to the part of the farm that faced the hillside. Hannah continued to trudge laboriously behind. She was obviously not fit. When she reached the top, she turned and looked at the sea below. There was only a narrow strip of sand and rocks between the house and the water. The house was high on the plot, which sloped sharply down to the shore.

"Do the waves ever reach the house?"

"No, at least they never have in the nearly twenty years I've lived here."

The rain started quickly and relentlessly, and Hannah cringed as the giant raindrops hit her face hard.

"It's often very windy out here, but don't worry, nothing will happen." Virginia took Hannah's arm and led her to an old door on the east side of the house. "That's my light barn!" Virginia proudly announced, flipping a switch to turn on the light. "The main house invites you to peace and time to enjoy life. But in this part of the farm, things happen, and problems get solved. Come inside!" Virginia stepped aside and let Hannah go in first.

Hannah walked cautiously into the barn, afraid that the ceiling might be as low as in the main house. To her relief, she found that the ceiling was very high, and she wouldn't bang her head against anything. She stopped in amazement at the sight before her. At least four meters to the ceiling, the old ceiling beams were exposed and painted in every color of the rainbow. The two long walls were decorated with beautiful patterns in bright colors, such as circles, waves, clouds, and trees. Despite the bright colors, the overall impression was incredibly calm and relaxing. Hannah had never seen anything like it.

At the end of the large room was a glass window that filled the entire wall. The window went from the floor to the ceiling—the light streaming in through the window and the roaring blue sea outside drew Hannah closer. Upon closer inspection, she saw that the big window was made of several smaller windows with almost invisible frames, giving the impression of one massive piece of glass. She noticed a pair of nearly invisible door handles that showed signs that opening part of the window was possible.

Hannah was wildly captivated by the beauty of the barn, and Virginia enjoyed seeing the young girl's changing facial expressions. The barn was furnished with small and large cushions, woolen blankets, and quilted rugs. There were pretty little tables of brass and old wood, and a large sofa stood against one wall. Hannah was impressed by the hundreds of different lamps in the barn. Small lamps, large lamps, brass lamps, lamps with glass shades, paper lamps, and one gorgeous lamp shaped like a giant abstract spiral. Some lamps stood on the floor or small tables, while others hung from the ceiling or were mounted on the walls. The result was uniquely beautiful. The many lamps emitted a stunningly bright light, so intense that it was almost overwhelming.

"It was a lot of work to make this all like you see it now, but I had a good friend who was an electrician, and we spent many hours planning how to set up the lights to make the most of the room." Virginia chuckled and flicked an almost hidden switch.

The previously bright light was now dim, glowing in a warm pinkish-gold tone, making everything look almost supernatural.

"The Farm on The Edge of The World is the most amazing place I've ever seen. It's a place where the light has all the power and where darkness never takes over. And believe me; it can get dark on a winter's night. The farm is completely isolated. The nearest other building is the old church right at the very tip of the headland. There is water on three sides of the church and only the cemetery faces land. By the way, it is a very beautiful cemetery, which is worth a visit." Virginia approached the large window as she spoke. "But no matter how dark it is, it's a good kind of darkness. It's the kind of dark that makes you appreciate the light more. The light barn is the most beautiful place on earth. When you stand there, and the light shines through the big windows and makes exciting shadows on the walls and the many different lamps glow each with their golden warm color, you know that everything is good. Or it will be very soon."

Hannah bent down and took off her socks. "The floor is so beautiful I have to feel it barefoot," she said, almost apologetically. "I've never seen a floor like this before." The stunning floor was a fabulous and enchanting mosaic of tiles in many sizes and shapes and every rainbow color.

An insistent scratching sound on the closed door made Virginia go over and open the door a tiny bit ajar.

Hannah looked at the door.

One ... two ... three ... five little striped kittens came shuffling in, followed by a majestic, chalky white cat with the longest tail Hannah had ever seen.

"It's the princess and her five little beauties," Virginia smiled, picking up the smallest kitten.

The beautiful white cat immediately approached Hannah and began wrapping her long tail around her legs.

Hannah bent down and stroked the cat gently, but was still mesmerized by her surroundings. "What do you use this amazing light barn for?"

"It's where I work," Virginia said, scratching the kitten behind the ear, so it began to purr loudly. "I need all the light. The darker everything feels, the more light it needs."

Hannah nodded; that made perfect sense. She knew all about trying desperately to get out of the darkness.

"I bathe in light—in the light of all colors. Warm white light, beautiful yellow light, bright golden light, faint bluish light, and best of all, the days when the sky is completely blue, and the sun is high, letting its life-giving rays shine down through the roof and in through the big windows. When the sun reaches into the farthest corners of the barn and throughout every inch of the building—those are the best days. The light from the water, the light from the sky, and the beautiful light that flickers through the trees in the forest and ends up here in my barn are all what make it so special. The light and warmth bring out my inner strength. The more light and warmth, the faster I think and solve my problems. The light makes me find the best possible solutions." Virginia farted merrily three or four times, so her skirt popped right out.

Hannah stood spellbound and let her eyes roam in an attempt to capture the beauty of the entire room at once. "The end wall is completely blank? How can that be?" Hannah looked at the creamy white, uneven wall that stood out starkly from the rest of the brightly colored walls. "Shouldn't there be a painting or something on that wall too?"

Virginia waved her hand to dissipate the smell of the last farts. "Oh yes, my sweet girl, but I wanted to wait until the right thing … or person … showed up." She looked at Hannah to see if she understood the meaning.

Hannah squinted her yellow-brown eyes and bit her lip. A low fart escaped between her buttocks. "Do you mean what I think you do?" She looked down at Virginia, eyes shining.

"Have you become a mind reader already?" Virginia smiled and sat on the built-in sofa arranged along one long wall. "But yes, I must admit I have been saving that wall for you. I meant to do something about it here in the spring, but I was hoping you'd come by and decorate the last empty wall in my light barn and make it perfect!"

Hannah slid down onto the couch and wrapped her arms around Virginia. "You're just so sweet." To her inner eye, she already saw a brilliant light portal—a light portal that shone with a crescendo of brightness. A feeling of intense awe ran through her, and she got goosebumps all over her body. "The light that lives forever…" she murmured.

Virginia smiled and settled more comfortably into the soft cushions, watching the young girl.

"What about your parents? Are they starting to take their responsibilities to you more seriously?" she asked.

Hannah shook her head. "I don't know. When I lived at home, my father was working a lot, and I regularly saw him with pretty young ladies." Hannah felt ashamed and didn't look at Virginia.

"That's his problem, not yours. You must never be ashamed of other people and their actions," Virginia replied reassuringly.

Hannah nodded thoughtfully and continued, "And Mom, I don't know what to say. I never felt like I had a mother. She never paid attention to me and didn't care about me from the day I started school. I remember a few times when I was a baby when my mother came to my room in the evening and stroked my hair before I fell asleep. But I never felt that my mother loved me. It was more like I was in the way. Almost as if I reminded her of something she didn't want to think about. Her life consisted of seeing how many young men she could get into her bed."

Hannah watched in amazement as a look of anger spread across Virginia's face—an expression she had never seen before.

"Could you have done anything to change that?" Virginia shook her head as if to clear her thoughts, and three hairpins flew out, landing on the beautiful mosaic floor.

"I don't think so." Hannah thoughtfully picked up one of the hairpins and began rubbing it between her fingers. "What could I have done?"

"Did you ever ask them why they didn't spend time with you?"

"No, I couldn't possibly ask that. My parents never showed any interest in me."

"If you don't ask, you won't get an answer, my sweet girl. And if you don't tell others how you feel, they can't know. You must tell them your thoughts, wishes, dreams, and feelings. And best of all, show them what you think. Most people understand best when they can see what you mean. Then they remember it much better. But enough about that for now. I don't have much left to tell you about the way your parents have treated you, and I'm sure you know that. But they were in your past, and now, you and I will look ahead, and I will teach you everything I know so you can learn how to handle any situation. And cheer up, my sweet girl, 'cause I have a little surprise planned for you. You'll have a special visitor arriving shortly."

"A visitor? Who would come out here just to see me?" Hannah thought for a second that her parents had decided to come all the way to the North Sea to visit their daughter.

"You remember I promised you that I'd get you some new clothes?"

"Clothes? Yes, I remember. You said you knew a lady who could sew."

"Yes, exactly, and she will come and visit you and take your measurements so you can get some clothes that fit your beautiful tall body." Virginia went and sat down in the rocking chair and one of the little striped kittens immediately jumped onto her lap.

Over the next few days, Hannah felt something change inside her. It wasn't just the new clothes that did it. Although it was nice to finally experience pants that were long enough and dresses that were the right length and covered her butt, the most important reason for her change was the certain knowledge that Virginia would support and guide her and prevent her from making mistakes. When she arrived, her back was bent and her head was bowed. But as the days passed, she found herself straightening up more and more, lifting her neck to look out over the horizon and the beautiful landscape.

Hannah couldn't help but notice that Virginia seemed happy to see her change. It made her feel good, like she was special.

Later that afternoon, Virginia was in the kitchen teaching Hannah how to make scones when there was a knock at the door.

"Open up, my sweet girl! I'm not expecting anyone, but it's always nice to have a visitor."

Hannah opened the door and was surprised to see an elderly man standing outside.

Without saying a word, he pushed her aside and walked into the kitchen to Virginia.

"Just step outside for a moment, my sweet girl." Virginia waved Hannah out and turned to face the angry man.

Hannah disappeared out the door, but not before she heard the man start yelling at Virginia.

"Who the hell is that big, tall girl staying on my farm?"

Hannah frowned and walked to the farthest corner of the courtyard, where she stayed until she saw the angry man leave. She smiled at him, but he just gave her a sour look and got on his moped and drove away.

Puzzled, Hannah went into the kitchen to Virginia. "Who was that man?"

"It was my neighbor, the farmer from the farm you can spot in the distance. He's having a hard time at the moment." Virginia didn't elaborate, but started shaping the dough into scones.

Chapter 12

The sandbank in the river was a lovely place, rarely flooded, and the river was still calm and steady, inviting beautiful swims.

"Did you sleep well, my sweet girl?" A few days after the farmer's visit, Virginia was up early and busy looking after the cats. "I slept really badly last night. I had the most ridiculous dreams." Hannah looked down at her bare feet, not wanting to meet Virginia's steady gaze. "It's a messed-up day today. Everything sucks." She popped a fart just to prove it was all crap.

"What nonsense, my sweet girl. There's no such thing as a lousy day. When you get up in the morning, start by being grateful for everything you already have, and then be grateful that it will be a beautiful day. Negative thoughts won't give you anything. But when you think positively, you CREATE a great day for yourself. You decide how you want to feel. So why not say to yourself … today, I choose to be happy! Today will be an awesome day! Can't you see it changes everything when you think that way?"

Hannah muttered and didn't answer, but asked a counter question. "What do you want me to do today?"

Virginia ignored her, lifted the thermos, and poured her a mug of coffee. "You look tired, my girl."

Hannah sighed, suddenly ashamed of being so cranky and unkind. "Those nightmares were awful. I was in a dark, gloomy maze, lost in countless long hallways and corridors. I looked for a way out and opened many doors to try to find an exit. But no matter which door I opened, it only led to a closed room."

"What was in those rooms?" Virginia regarded her thoughtfully. "Could you see anything, or was it dark?"

"All the rooms were lit, and I could see they were empty. I could only see big black letters on the white end wall."

"Ah." Virginia knowingly took a sip of her hot coffee. "Letters, you say. Did the words make sense, or was it pure gibberish to you?"

"They didn't make sense. Not a single one of them. I was saddened and sorry because I hadn't learned everything I should have."

"You will. You'll learn everything you need to."

Hannah returned to describing her dream. "The last room I opened was different. It wasn't empty."

"What was in there?"

"Not what, but who. YOU were in there. You stood in the far corner, looked at me, and said, 'Remember to begin at the beginning.'"

"Do you understand the meaning?"

Hannah bit her lower lip, as she often did when she thought intensely. "Yes, I think I do, actually." She looked at Virginia, and a small smile played about her mouth. "You told me to start at the beginning. I have to read and learn before I understand what the different letters mean."

"You're smart, my sweet girl. That's exactly what that dream means. Tell me how it ended. What's the last thing you remember before you woke up?"

"I wanted to see you, but you came and slammed the door in my face. I started crying, and when I woke up, my pillow was wet with my tears. I was devastated."

"Who are you grieving for?" Virginia asked softly, taking her hand.

"You know very well what has happened in my life. I have every reason to grieve." Hannah pulled her hand away. She was not at all ready to stop grieving.

"What happened in the past doesn't need your grief. That's why I think you're grieving for yourself." Virginia grabbed a bag of cat food and smiled as all the cats immediately stood with their tails lifted, ready to pounce on the food.

She continued, "When a wanderer gets a thorn in his foot, he pulls it out if he's smart. Only a fool lets it sit and says: 'I will keep this thorn to prick me so I may always remember the pain.'"

Hannah looked at Virginia with tears in her eyes.

"Believe me, it's always better to remember with joy than sorrow and pain." Virginia squeezed Hannah's shoulder before quietly walking back into the courtyard and closing the door behind her.

Hannah sighed and followed her outside.

"I'm sorry; I didn't mean to be angry and ungrateful."

"It's okay, I understand."

"I don't know what was wrong, but when I woke up this morning, I was in a bad mood, and that dream wouldn't let me go. But I promise to start believing in myself and keep studying and learning to be as clever as you."

"Just as the clouds come and go and change shape, color, and size, so do your thoughts. Just wait; you'll accomplish much more than I ever have. You're going to help thousands of people. Help them find their own path to happiness. Help them understand what's important to them and opt out of everything that doesn't matter much, even if it's what other people think leads to happiness."

"Do you really think I can do all that?"

"Not yet, but I'm proud of you, and you'll get there one day. Look." Virginia pointed to a small inconspicuous bird high in the sky. "It's a lark. It flies in spirals, and with each spiral, it sings louder and louder and becomes more and more filled with joy. It is one of the first signs of spring, long before the trees and flowers bloom."

Hannah squinted her eyes. It was hard to see, but she could clearly hear the happy trills of the little bird.

"You must never let your thoughts limit you. You can only see as far ahead as you can think." Virginia smiled and continued, "Try saying instead—'I live in the moment and look forward to solving any challenge that comes my way.'"

Hannah smiled. "Yeah, I can see how it's more positive to focus on how you can have a good day instead of spending energy feeling sorry for yourself and getting stuck in the mindset that everything sucks." She had never talked to another human being about these things before. It was new territory for her, but she enjoyed every moment and soaked up Virginia's knowledge and experience.

"Remember, my girl, I don't know everything; there is so much I haven't had time to learn. When I was young, there were not the same opportunities as now. Back then, it was difficult to find books on the subjects that interested me, and you couldn't just use the internet for information like you can now. You have access to all the greatest in each field, and if you use them correctly, you will become one of them one day—one of those who others listen to and draw knowledge from. You will become immortal."

"I'm not clever enough to do all that."

Virginia looked at her sternly. "It's not who you are that keeps you from achieving your goals. It's always who you think you're not. You don't think you're good enough because you haven't had that many successes yet. We'll change that very soon. Small steps in the right direction are much better than seven-mile steps in the wrong one!"

Hannah nodded thoughtfully. "So, when do you reach your goals?"

"Sometimes it's quick, and other times it takes longer. Maybe even a very long time. But you always succeed when you believe in and act on it, taking small steps in the right direction daily."

Hannah tiptoed and reached for a ladybug perched on the thatch. The ladybug immediately crawled onto her finger, and she held it up, watching the beautiful red insect before blowing on it and letting it fly back into the sky.

Virginia smiled. "Never dismiss an idea, dream, or goal because you feel it will be difficult and take a long time. If you want to achieve your goals and succeed in what you choose, you have to expect it to be hard work." Virginia turned red in the face and squeezed out a fart.

"It sounded like it was hard work too!" Hannah grinned and continued, "But I understand what you're saying, and I'll be firm and stick it out. No giving up halfway through."

"That's good, my sweet girl. Just remember that as long as you are true to yourself and work at exactly what you want to do, it doesn't matter how many hours, days, weeks, months, and years you have to put in. It will always be worth it."

Hannah hugged her, picked up a hairpin, and rubbed it.

"Nothing in the world can replace perseverance. Just look at our little kittens." Virginia smiled at the little wooly tots scampering about, chasing each other. "When a cat wants something, you can be sure it will get it. It won't stop until it has succeeded. If it has to try a hundred times to reach the bird's nest, it will. If it wants your attention, it will keep circling you, meowing, or getting in the way of your legs. Cats often achieve their goals. They rarely give up halfway."

Hannah smiled and watched the princess wrap her long tail around the smallest of the kittens in an attempt to keep it close. The little kitten, munching and chewing, got loose and leaped gleefully into the tall grass to chase a butterfly.

"I see what you mean. Aren't there books that describe it in a little more detail?"

"Sure, come on in." Virginia went to the bookcase and took out a thick book. "Read this. You can learn a lot from it."

"It's in English." Hannah held the old book out to Virginia, who shook her head.

"Keep it. And yes, it is in English, but you have studied English in school and spent a few weeks in New York. I'm sure you will pick it up quickly. You must be able to read English; it's essential for your future development. If you don't understand the English language, you limit yourself too much."

"Do you read English books?" Hannah flipped through the old book, which bore the mark of being read over and over again throughout many years. The brown cover was faded and worn, with creases along the edges. She opened the book and discovered that the pages were yellowed and stained, and that there were quite a lot of dog-ears on the pages. There were several handwritten notes and underlined passages throughout the book that had obviously highlighted important or interesting sections.

Virginia nodded. "Yes, I learned the language when I was your age."

Hannah was curious. There were so many questions about Virginia's life that she wanted answers to. But so far, she hadn't succeeded. But maybe the time was better now.

"You've never been married?"

Virginia didn't answer, and Hannah took that as a no.

"Have you never been in love either?"

Virginia nodded. "Well, once, a very long time ago." She didn't elaborate, and as she turned on the faucet and began washing the fresh seaweed she had just retrieved from the shore, Hannah realized there were just some questions she wasn't going to get answered.

And every single time Virginia had visitors and showed them into the light barn, Hannah asked if she could sit with them and listen.

"Later, my sweet girl, you will be allowed to join in, but you are not quite ready yet. Why don't you go for a little walk, and now that you have learned to swim so well, why don't you go for a swim? The weather is lovely today."

Hannah walked slowly down towards the beach. She really wished she would be allowed to watch when Virginia was working. And she had a strange feeling that it had to be soon; soon so as not to end up being late.

⁓

Over the next few months, Hannah seemingly evolved from an insecure teenager to a grown woman. Now she finally had a path she could follow. She set off along the course, not knowing the prize or the distance, yet she followed it joyfully, putting her whole soul into it.

This day she was lying in a dune with a pile of books beside her. Hannah was born to help other people. That was just the way it was. It was still a long way off, but Virginia felt pride that she was the one who had set that process in motion. A process that would never stop.

"You will go far, my sweet girl. I just know that." Virginia watched Hannah as she read, thoughtfully scratching the back of her neck where a mosquito had found rest.

Hannah looked up from her book in surprise. "Why do you think I will be able to do that?"

"You've been through so much already, but you're still curious and willing to learn and you don't doubt yourself."

Hannah read quickly because she knew that one day she would come back and reread it all. After all, this was just reconnaissance into the unknown land of the mind and how to use common sense to achieve your goals. Hannah looked at the titles. *Unlock Your True Potential… Destiny Is a Choice… Happy High Status…* All exciting books that described how to develop and become *someone*. Hannah knew that she had to become *someone* first, and only then could she start thinking about what she wanted to be. Books about how to become *something*.

It still amazed her how quickly she got used to reading books in English. But that was no doubt because she was reading about something that really interested her.

While she still had her eyes on the book, she reached into her pocket and pulled out a pen, underlining a sentence she wanted to return to. Then she went on, and after a short while, she used the pen frequently.

"No," she wrote somewhere in the margin. "Good," she wrote somewhere else.

Virginia gave her a warm smile and patted her on the shoulder.

Hannah suddenly saw something in Virginia's eyes that she had never seen before. It took her a moment to realize it was admiration. Virginia is proud of *me*. She believes in *me*. That made her feel good inside and she continued reading, and as she flipped through the book, she realized that she was starting to form her own opinions and thoughts about what she was reading.

"When you really start to understand everything you read, you will realize that you can go far in life." Virginia let out a little fart of joy. "In fact, there are no limits except the ones you create. But we'll talk more about that later, when you've learned even more. But I want you to know that it makes me very happy to see how talented you are. Part of it is because you've already had so many painful experiences in your short life. But fortunately, they have not destroyed you, and together we two will make you strong so that you can find yourself and your path along the River of Life. After all, you are not supposed to just barely stay afloat. It's much more fun to take control and steer the journey yourself."

Hannah put the book down and walked carefully around a large beetle crawling in the grass. She looked at her feet to avoid stepping on one of the many creatures that scurried and crawled about. She came to look at her long slender feet with the extra-long number two toe. Considering her height, her feet weren't that big. But of course, they were a lot bigger than Virginia's. Hannah glanced over at Virginia, who was dozing in a hammock with her eyes closed for a rare moment. She walked closer. It was not often that she had the opportunity to look at Virginia when she was doing nothing. Virginia looked peaceful and happy and Hannah felt a warm feeling inside. A feeling of belonging with her. She moved her gaze from Virginia's face to her feet. Funny, she had an extra-long number two toe too. Otherwise, her feet were small and stout, but the toes themselves resembled her own.

Hannah went to play with the cats. She laughed out loud with delight when the striped kitten jumped into her arms and began to purr loudly.

Virginia sat up in the hammock and looked over at the sound. The young girl's brown eyes shone warmly, and there were mysterious shadows in those magic eyes. Eyes that testified to superior intelligence and something else that gave Virginia goosebumps all over.

As a butterfly fluttered by, Hannah watched with fascination as Virginia raised her hand. The butterfly landed on her index finger, and Hannah approached cautiously.

"Come here, my dear. Hold out your hand," Virginia said. Hannah reached out her right hand, and Virginia gently placed the butterfly on it.

"Take a good look at it, Hannah. Isn't it a lovely butterfly?" Virginia smiled at her.

"Yes, I love all the butterflies and animals out here," Hannah replied.

"Blow gently on the butterfly," Virginia instructed. Hannah blew, and the butterfly took off, flying around them before darting towards the forest.

"That was strange," Hannah murmured.

"I live in harmony with nature, my dear. The animals know I mean them no harm," Virginia explained.

"You can't be mean to something so beautiful," Hannah said, breaking wind and sitting down on the grass.

"It takes time for a butterfly to unfold its wings. They're not born with beautiful wings," Virginia said, patting her hand. "Remember, everything takes time."

Hannah nodded. "I understand."

Virginia pointed to a pot of red flowers. "The flowers don't wait for the bees to come. They burst into full bloom, emitting their fragrance and attracting the bees."

Hannah nodded again.

"It's the same with life's challenges. Don't wait for miracles—create them yourself and know you will succeed. If the flowers could talk, they would tell you the same. They know the bees will come when they show their full potential."

"I don't know what my potential is," Hannah said, feeling inadequate.

"That's what we're working on. When the time is right, you'll find your way. Remember, thoughts are just thoughts. Thoughts come and go, and you decide which ones to act on and which to let go."

Hannah smiled and pursed her lips and blew as hard as she could.

"Don't waste time on negative thoughts. Focus on the things you want and let go of everything else. Look at the flower bed. See all the bees? If one lands on you, what do you do?"

"I gently wave the bee away because I don't want it there." She began to understand what Virginia meant. "You mean I should do the same with my thoughts?"

"Yes, think of the things you don't want or the people you don't want in your life as a bug you want to remove. But always do it in a good and orderly way. Never hard and brutal."

Hannah didn't hear the last of what Virginia said. Her quick brain had already begun to think ahead. Couldn't something clever be developed that people could quickly learn to use? Perhaps it would be possible to draw her thoughts. "Can I paint another picture on the end wall in the light barn? I know I said I was done a long time ago, but I just had a good idea." Hannah looked hopefully at Virginia, having risen from the hammock and now standing with two cats in her arms, both vying to get the most attention.

"Of course, you may. I told you I was saving that wall for you. I want it to reflect your talent!"

⁂

Hannah walked to the end wall of the light barn and stood in front of it, looking at what she had painted the day before. Her cheeks turned red, and her eyes sparkled. Even the thick dark brown hair seemed alive as she craned her neck.

"You have done a beautiful job on that wall. I am so proud of you. I may not know much about art, but I like what I see."

Hannah smeared a bright red color on the wall and said, "I try to find my own style without being influenced too much by other artists. But I don't know if I've succeeded."

"It's very beautiful and I've never seen anything like it. You can be proud." Virginia took a few steps back and watched her work from a distance.

Hannah pointed to the part of the wall she had painted the day before. "What do you think I called that painting?"

"A woman's face—a circle—a spiral, and then some beautiful butterflies." Virginia looked first at each part of the picture. "Your pictures always symbolize something. So, I wonder if it's called 'Spread Your Wings.'"

"Close! I will call it 'The Spiral's Wings.'"

"Good title." Virginia asked a question she seemed to be thinking about for a while. "Do you want to sell your pictures?"

"Well, they're not good enough for anyone to buy them. Do you really think some people would pay money for my pictures?"

Virginia smiled. "What do you think?"

Hannah shook her head. "I don't know."

"What do you think of your last picture? Are you happy with it?"

"Yeah, it turned out exactly how I wanted it."

"So, don't you think there are other people who share your opinion?"

"Yes, you're right." Hannah hugged her and didn't blink as Virginia presented a huge fart.

Hannah's technical painting skills were improving. She was constantly trying new things in a playful, experimental way. The result was an exciting product of her unique imagination, intuition, and emotional power.

When she painted, she could always hear Virginia saying, "Try to visualize exactly what you dream of. Draw it in every detail."

Hannah concentrated on the image she saw in her mind's eye. After all, she had promised Virginia a light portal on the part of the wall, 'The Light That Lives Forever,' and of course, it had to be perfect. Virginia believed in her so unconditionally that Hannah never doubted herself again.

"You are my rudder." Hannah left the brushes and walked to the built-in couch where Virginia was relaxing with a book. "You steer me safely through any trouble that comes my way." Hannah laid her head in Virginia's lap and looked up at her gentle face. "You know, I often used to dream of the river and how I was rushing down it at breakneck speed, completely out of control."

"Yes, my girl, you've told me that several times."

"I haven't felt like that while I've been here with you. In all the time I've been here with you, I haven't dreamed that disgusting dream about the raging river. The river I can't control, the river that just takes me here and there and exposes me to all sorts of unpleasant things."

Hannah lay in the hammock and looked at the sky, which was covered in dark, perilous clouds. They were all shades of gray, and they looked gloomy, just like her thoughts at the moment. She tried with all her might to think positive thoughts, but they kept returning to the past—to the nasty years at school, the years with Anders, and all the terrible things that happened then. Her thoughts stopped when she reached the day she lost her unborn child. Those thoughts were too heavy to bear.

She closed her eyes and tried to make the gloomy thoughts go away, but she was unsuccessful. When she opened her eyes again, she saw that the sky had changed. Where it had been all gray, almost black, just a few minutes ago, there were suddenly large gaps of bright blue between all the clouds. The beautiful blue sky was pushing away the dark clouds. This was exactly what she had just tried to do with her thoughts. The sky was obviously better at it than she was, but it had also had millennia to practice.

Hannah smiled. That probably meant she needed to practice to control her thoughts better. She let out a few tiny, relatively silent farts and suddenly remembered one of Virginia's favorite phrases: "The sooner you make decisions and act on them, the sooner you will find yourself changing and getting closer to your goals and dreams."

At that moment, Hannah realized she had started acting and thinking differently, that she was gradually gaining more and more control over her life. She felt that she had learned so much but, at the same time, was fully aware of how little she really knew.

Hannah turned away from the sky and looked at the open landscape. Far out on the horizon was the old village church; even farther out, she could just make out the neighboring farm.

It was odd because, with so few neighbors, you'd think you'd get along with the ones you had. But on the occasions when she had seen the old farmer, he had turned away without greeting her. She also never saw him welcome Virginia.

She rose from her hammock and walked to the slope's edge, her eyes again wandering to the water. There was a myriad of blue colors—blue sky and blue water. The water was flat for once without white foam tops.

A group of people walked by down on the beach. They were nudging each other and started laughing when they spotted Hannah up on the edge. Two men bowed and waved at her, making funny faces.

Hannah sighed. It was the same every time. She was so tired of being made fun of.

One of the young men waved and made a motion with his hands that showed he had noticed her large breasts. The others laughed and started waving at her too, and suddenly she realized that it wasn't her they were laughing at! They were laughing because they were happy, and they were laughing because they were alive. They were not teasing *her*. They would have teased any other woman they had passed. It had nothing to do with her as a person. For the first time, she fully understood that it was possible to tease without being mean and personal.

Hannah couldn't help but burst into a chuckle that quickly turned into a real laugh, and before she knew it, she let out a huge fart. Hell, she was alive too! She felt the beginnings of arousal spread from her heart and out into her fingers and down to her toes until it engulfed her completely. She was alive again! She felt good. She looked forward to a new day with new tasks, challenges, solutions, joy, laughter, and problems to be solved. The memory of all the bad experiences, failures, pain, and death would always be in her, but now it was not a sickening torment. She had taken out a thorn.

Her whole body filled with a joy she had not previously experienced. It tingled down to her extra-long second toe. She only returned to reality when a loud sound disturbed her thoughts. A car came driving up the dusty dirt road, and Hannah walked into the courtyard to see if it was someone she knew.

Chapter 13

The river grew muddy and murky, and the water rose slowly.

A small black car pulled into the courtyard, and a fat man climbed out of the driver's seat with difficulty. Hannah looked at the man with interest. His size made it impossible for him to stand up straight due to his bulging belly.

"Over here." Hannah waved at him. She assumed without further ado that he was one of those who came to seek Virginia's help.

Virginia always showed new guests to the light barn, and Hannah waited on the doorstep, ready to show the fat man inside.

"Is it true that Virginia can read people? I live farther south but I have heard about her, and her skills." William looked at the cozy courtyard with the many flower pots and didn't dare meet Hannah's gaze as he continued. "I have heard that she is often able to tell what a problem is, just by observing and understanding with her heart, so that one doesn't have to make long, difficult explanations." There was something hopeful in his voice that did not escape Hannah's attention.

She nodded. "Yes, there are several people who believe that and I know that Virginia is very talented and very, very sweet and understanding. So I'm sure she can help you too."

Before William had time to answer, Virginia entered the courtyard while buttoning the last buttons of her pretty blue dress. "No, my sweet girl. He's my private guest." Virginia gave the man a beaming smile. "Hello, you must be William. Come on—this way." To Hannah's surprise, Virginia then led the man into her bedroom!

Hannah chuckled. Virginia was not going to work with the fat man at all, it was pure pleasure. Of course, there had to be time for that, and Virginia wasn't old, only in her mid-fifties.

The curtain in Virginia's bedroom window was drawn, and Hannah decided that a long walk on the beach would be a good idea.

⁓

Hannah didn't get back in the house until the black car had driven off again. In the kitchen, she was greeted by a smiling and energetic Virginia, who was busy cleaning clams.

"Who was that vast man?" Hannah's curiosity got the better of her, even though she had decided not to ask.

"It was William. He's a lovely and nice man. Very lonely and eccentric and has mental problems because he's so big."

"How do you get so fat? He must eat all the time."

"He eats the same things you did, except he doesn't throw up his food." Virginia held her gaze.

"Did you know I threw up after I ate?" Hannah looked embarrassed.

"Of course, you had marks on your hand, and any idiot could figure out that you would develop an eating disorder when you were with someone who kept saying you were fat."

"It is so strange. When I was with Anders, I felt that it was necessary for me to throw up every time I ate. And every time I threw up, I felt a little better for a while. But then you came to visit me in the hospital and were so sweet and loving and listened to me.

I could feel that you were genuinely interested in my well-being, and suddenly I no longer felt the need to throw up. I remember there was a brochure on eating disorders on my bedside table, but I didn't even have to look at it. The problem simply didn't exist anymore. It was wonderful. Your loving care cured me. I'm so grateful."

"You are on the right path now, my sweet girl, and I will do my part to make sure William gets there too."

"Do you know why he eats so much? Do you already know what his problem is?"

Virginia smiled cheekily. "Yes, I do. He was a virgin at the age of forty-nine! He had never known the joy of having sex. But I put an end to that, I can tell you!"

Hannah gasped. "Did you say sex?"

"Yes, of course. We had great sex. William will return in a few days, and then we'll continue the lesson. That helps me, too, of course. Good sex makes me feel high all day! You should try it!"

"Should I find someone to have sex with?" Hannah gasped. "Are you telling me this even though you know how Anders treated me?"

Virginia shrugged and flicked a fart, which neither of them noticed. "You're not quite ready to find yourself a boyfriend yet. But that doesn't mean you can't have sex. You can start by having sex with yourself!"

Hannah was speechless. "Give myself an orgasm? Do you mean I have to fiddle with myself down there?"

"Yes, that's perfectly natural. The best way when you need to soothe yourself is a brisk little clitoral orgasm. A quiet clitoral orgasm does wonders for your mental and physical well-being." Virginia said it the same way she would have if she had asked Hannah to feed the cats. Quite naturally, quite calmly.

"I can't do that."

"Sex with yourself is nothing to be afraid of or have any old-fashioned taboo about. You need to know your body and its reactions before guiding your lover. Men often need a little help. Certainly, not all of them can figure it out completely without help. Too often, they think that what they have between their legs is enough to satisfy a woman, but it takes much more."

That resonated with her, and Hannah nodded. She already knew that because she had never been satisfied by Anders, and he had undoubtedly had something between his legs.

Virginia continued, "Nah, see. Men often need a little loving guidance before it gets perfect."

Hannah had a hard time imagining that sex could be great.

"Common sense isn't sexy and nice girls never get any!" Virginia looked at Hannah with a small, subtle smile. "That's just the way it is. I've said it, and now it's up to you to use or forget that knowledge. But you'd do well to get out on the road of life. You need to experience how wonderful it is to be sexually satisfied. It doesn't have to be someone you marry, just a nice guy who can show you that men can be kind." Virginia laughed and added, "Sex is actually quite nice."

"Is sex nice?" That was not how she had experienced it, neither with Anders nor Simon.

Virginia looked at her appraisingly for a moment before she reached into the pocket of her dress and took out a folded piece of paper. "Read my notes, my sweet girl, if you are interested in understanding what sex should be like. It must always be a nice and wonderful experience. Whether it is gentle or more hardcore sex is entirely up to the participants, but sex must be a two-way experience to be really great."

Within hours of receiving Virginia's notes, Hannah decided to go for a walk. She disappeared down to the beach and sat in a secluded sandpit. She hesitated for a moment before she unfolded Virginia's notes and began to read. Was she ready to read about sex? Hadn't she had enough sex already? An inner voice immediately popped up and she heard it as clearly as if someone was standing in front of her shouting it. *You need to learn that sex can be great. You must not shut down that part of your life. If you do, your journey along the River of Life will never be complete.* Hannah sighed and started reading.

> *It didn't take me long to realize what the problem was. It was all in his head. He was afraid of women. It was obvious to me, and I asked him if he had ever had sex with a woman and he told me that he had tried once, but it hadn't worked out at all.*
>
> *I knew immediately how to help him. I made him sit down on the bed next to me and calmly told him to just relax and do as I asked. I could see that he was scared and uncomfortable and I smiled at him and stroked his hair. For a long time, we sat next to each other on the bed and chatted about anything and everything before I sensed a change in him. He began to relax.*
>
> *I sensed that he was ready for us to move on and I told him what was going to happen. I tried to hold his gaze as I licked my lower lip, with a sensual movement. I moved my gaze to his crotch and could see that it was affecting him and I asked him to sit still as I gently started touching him on the outside of his pants.*
>
> *I must admit that there was something about his insecurity that turned me on tremendously and I was happy when I sensed that he was ready for the next step.*

I helped him get undressed and took off my own clothes and told him that I needed him. I told him that I liked that he was a big man. That he should never be ashamed of his body.

He stared enchanted at my breasts, but suddenly I could see that he was once again insecure and he tried to pull away.

Such a cute little wee-wee. Don't worry; it will grow big and hard again. As I said this, I could feel him relaxing again and I knew he was just about ready for his first intercourse.

I started using my hands on his little pecker, making my voice deep and enticing. The faster I worked, the calmer he became. Suddenly I could feel that he was ready. I could feel him stop struggling and surrender to the rapid movements of my hands.

Once he had surrendered, it was quick. His little pecker got bigger and bigger and finally so hard that I could tell he was ready for me.

I made him lie down on his back so that I could ride him. It was the easiest position when his belly was so big. I told him that I needed him and that he was doing well. I told him that he was so big and hard, and that was the last thing he needed to hear before he started moving inside me.

I could clearly feel his passion growing and I must admit I enjoyed it very much. And it was a pleasure for me to see how a previously shy and insecure man suddenly became brave and confident just because he experienced the pleasure of satisfying a woman.

I started moving faster and faster and before long we both exploded in a huge firework of pleasure.

Afterwards, I lay down on the bed next to him and held him and told him how important it is for a woman to be caressed after sex. I told him that a woman wants to feel loved and appreciated and that the moment right after sex was absolutely fantastic if you wanted to establish a close relationship.

I explained to him that there was nothing to be afraid of and I could see that he understood. He will never again be afraid of having sex with a woman.

He told me that he had never before experienced such a feeling of deep and great peace and he pressed his face between my breasts and said that he wanted to lie like that forever.

It was really nice and I told him so and we agreed to meet and have sex again very soon.

Hannah slowly folded the paper and placed it in the pocket of her dress. Virginia had certainly given her something to think about and she already had a feeling that what she had just read would turn out to be a very important lesson.

Chapter 14

The waters of the river were replenished, increasing their volume, and eating away at the sandbank day by day, making the formerly safe sandbank an unsafe place to be.

The sky to the east was absolutely stunning. The dawning sunshine pushed through the cloud formations and transformed them into wild, bright colors and shapes, turning the clouds into the most beautiful dream images. Hannah sniffed in, enjoying the sea's spicy scent and the big pines' warm crispness. She turned and stared at the ocean. Seagulls, out for an early breakfast, dipped low over the water, cutting into the silence with their lonely cries. The scent of flowers, a tribute to spring, floated softly on the breeze.

She loved the early morning walks along the water. They not only gave her peace of mind, but also energized her. It was as if the energy found all within nature would seep directly into her pores. She had never felt more at ease anywhere than here, on the farm with Virginia. Hannah gathered fresh green seaweed as she walked, and when there was enough for dinner, she climbed the slope happily and energetically and disappeared into the kitchen.

"Oops." Hannah clutched her head. "Wouldn't you think I would have learned by now that the doors are too low for me? After all, I've been here for a year and a half."

In all the time Hannah had been on the farm, her height hadn't bothered her, except when she was in a hurry and forgot to duck her head and popped it into one of the low doorways or one of the exposed ceiling beams in the farmhouse.

Virginia, being so tiny herself, had never once made her feel different. This made it especially hard when the nice middle-aged man who used to deliver groceries every Thursday had become ill and a thin lady with a shrill voice had taken over his route.

"That's weird how tall you are! How can you be so abnormally tall? It shouldn't be allowed. You look like an alien!" The lady glared at Hannah unabashedly as she unloaded the goods and placed them in the yard at a proper distance from Hannah.

"I can't help it if I'm tall, but you can help it if you're rude." Hannah forgot everything she'd been taught about not caring about other people's comments and huffed.

"That's a terrible temper you have, though." The lady glared sourly at Hannah as she got into the car and drove away.

"Holy shit, what a bitch!" Hannah looked at Virginia for approval.

Virginia shook her head. "Never waste your energy on what others think or say about you. You better keep your mouth shut if you can't say something nice. Never be provoked into reacting like that."

"What should I do then?"

"You must repay her rudeness with kindness and politeness."

"Even when she behaves like that and calls me an alien?"

"Yes, of course. If you answer back, then you both lose. If you take it in stride and answer back politely, you win. And when you get really good at answering back the right way, you both win!" Virginia scratched her hair with a hairpin and placed it on the table. "Look around. Nature always talks to us, but unfortunately, only a few people know how to listen. Nature sends us little messages, reminding us that it's time to stop, move on, relax, believe that everything will be okay, and to live in the moment. Listening to the environment and learning from the animals is common sense. They always use their instincts and are not controlled by what other animals think about them."

"Sorry. I know, but I forgot…"

"We're only human, my sweet girl. We can never be one hundred percent successful at what we do. We will always make mistakes."

"You haven't." Hannah looked down adoringly at Virginia's calm face.

"Oh yes, my girl, I certainly have." An expression of great sadness suddenly appeared on the otherwise happy face. "I have had my share of mistakes in life, and I still make mistakes. In fact, I'm not sure if I recently made one of the biggest mistakes of my life."

"Oh, I'm sorry to hear that."

"That's okay, my girl, but I feel it's time to go to the light barn and work. This time by myself! It's time for a soul walk!"

"Soul walk? You have never told me about that before. Can I join you?"

"Soul walk is my most powerful tool. But unfortunately, you're not ready for it … not yet, anyway." Virginia shook her head. "A walk like that always leaves me exhausted and unable to move for hours afterward. I only use it when absolutely necessary. I usually get a bad nosebleed afterward and lie on the floor like I'm about to give up on life. But it always gives me knowledge. The knowledge I couldn't get any other way. Soul walking is something unique. I first heard about it about ten years ago, and I've developed and refined it to suit me very well," Virginia explained.

"It sounds fascinating!"

"When I feel you're ready for it, I'll teach you and make you a great soul walker." Virginia let out a little fart.

"Okay." Hannah looked disappointed.

"I suggest you take a long walk instead. All the way to the cemetery or even farther. You're ready to start using all that knowledge I've been cramming into your head for several months."

"Use?"

"Yes, find some people who speak to you, speak to your innermost self. People who need a little bit of your common sense. Use what you've learned here at The Farm on The Edge of The World."

Hannah put on a pair of old sneakers and headed toward the church. It was a beautiful day, and something made her want to continue past the church, where she would usually turn around and head back. She had never been this far before. A few miles past the church was a farm, and even farther out was the town.

Hannah walked briskly on her long legs, humming a happy little tune as she went—nature really did energize her. She reached the farm and stopped for a moment. The big farm looked neat and well-kept. It must be the old farmer she had seen a few times before who lived there. She had only just finished thinking about it when he rode past on his moped. She waved at him, but he looked at her sourly, as usual, and drove on without saying hello.

Hannah walked on along the fence. Before she knew it, she was near the small town. She had only been there once, on the day she arrived by train and took a taxi to the farm. The woods stretched all along her right, and suddenly her keen ears caught something happening inside the woods. Without hesitation, she set off running. A group of children were teasing a young, skinny guy who seemed to be a couple of years older than them. The young guy was sitting on the ground and crying.

They stopped as she approached. There was silence, other than the sound of the young boy sobbing. One of the other boys came right up to Hannah, confident and defensive.

"You're really tall."

"Nah, I just wore the long legs today!"

"You are tall," a little girl with braces on her teeth interjected.

"Really? I didn't know that!"

"You must know." The oldest of the boys glared at her.

Hannah smiled and shook her head. "Am I tall? I didn't realize it."

The smallest of the boys looked her up and down. "I want to be as tall as you!"

"Yes, I understand that. It's pretty cool to be tall." Hannah realized in amazement that she actually meant it! She was beginning to feel that being so tall was a good thing.

"What are you doing here?" A little girl with pigtails and bare toes in tiny gold sandals stared at her unabashedly.

"Have you ever experienced an earthquake?" Hannah grinned inwardly.

"There are no earthquakes in Denmark." The oldest boy stared at her superiorly.

"Yes, there certainly are, and I can feel a dangerous one coming on right now." As Hannah spoke, she turned around so that her butt was right at head height with the kids. A mega, gigantic fart was being squeezed out of her butt at record speed, and the sound was ear-splitting. "Now that's what I call an earthquake! At least eight on the fart scale!"

The girl with the pigtails started laughing, and suddenly they were all laughing, and the more they laughed, the funnier it got until finally, they sank onto the soft foliage of the forest floor, exhausted.

"That's the loudest fart I've EVER heard," the oldest boy said, deeply impressed. "How is it that you can make such an enormous fart?"

"It's because I have a tight butthole! The tighter the butthole, the louder the farts. So, my butthole is in top shape!"

With loud laughter, the children disappeared, and Hannah was suddenly alone with the thin young man.

"Hi," she smiled kindly at him. When he didn't respond, she sat beside him. "I'm Hannah. What's your name?"

"Noah," he mumbled, looking down at his shoes. Hannah followed his glance and smiled. He was wearing running shoes, the largest shoes she had ever seen!

"What are you upset about?" Hannah asked.

"They're always teasing me."

Hannah nodded. "I know all about that. I was always teased at school because I was always so tall. What do they tease you about?"

"My big feet."

"It must be great to have big feet! They should be used for something!" Hannah thought for a moment. "Don't you think you'd be good at running marathons?" She looked at his slim body. "I read about how it's important not to weigh too much."

"Run a marathon? How could I possibly do that?"

"If you really want to, I'm sure it's possible. I don't know much about running, but I spent a year and a half learning how to set goals for myself and how to achieve them."

Noah looked at her with interest. "Can you tell me more about it?"

"Of course, I will." Hannah noticed a sparkle in his eyes that hadn't been there before.

"I already know what not to do." Noah gave her a wry smile. "When I was in seventh grade, I had a bad experience. We had to run 1,500 meters, and I was in shape and thinking that it would be a piece of cake. I started to run fast, but totally died out after a few hundred meters."

"What went wrong?"

"I started way too hard."

"So, you haven't run at all since?"

He shook his head. "No, I got a bad feeling about running from that."

Hannah had a strange feeling that something else had contributed to the negative feeling. "Do you have a girlfriend?" She would guess he was a year or two younger than herself, so it would be only natural.

"No!" He shook his head and asked quickly, "What about you? Have you ever run a race?"

Hannah felt like there was something he didn't want to tell her, but she immediately accepted that he had changed the subject.

"No, I've never run a race and don't want to, though I might be good at running with the long legs I'm equipped with." She smiled and continued, "If you want to run a marathon, you should. If you think it would be cool to complete the proverbial distance, then you should do it."

Noah got up and ran around a bit. "I haven't thought about it before, but I actually think it's something I'd like to do."

"Then go for it! The limiting factor is rarely the body but more often the head. It should never be something you do 'because you have to run a marathon' or 'because it's cool to have completed a marathon.' There should be a burning desire to do it. Why you want to run doesn't matter, but there must be a sincere desire to do it. A desire so strong that it overcomes all obstacles on the way to the finish."

Noah nodded. "I understand that, and I'm also well aware that the foundations have to be in place. You have to be in shape. You have to control your strength and your fluid intake along the way."

"One day, you'll run a marathon! I know you will, and I'd love to talk to you again sometime. You are welcome to visit me at The Farm on The Edge of The World." She waved at him and happily walked away.

Her brown eyes shone with joy, and she felt good about herself. She stopped and looked at some magnificent mushrooms of a sort she had never seen before. As she lifted her eyes and let them wander over the stunning landscape, she was reminded how extraordinary life was and how important it was to enjoy every moment and always make the most of it.

Hannah went on in deep thought, while at the same time letting the sun and light penetrate and stimulate all her senses. She reached the cemetery in a marvelous state of mind of intense inner joy and anticipation.

A small, burly man standing next to a beautiful old jar of brightly colored flowers caught her eye, and she stopped. Could he be one of those who needed a little common sense? She closed her eyes and stood still for almost a minute before resolutely walking over to stand before him.

"Good afternoon. Pretty flowers you have there." Hannah held out her hand and said, "I'm Hannah, and you?"

The man pretended not to hear her.

Hannah stood right in front of him and straightened to her full height.

"You're blocking the sun."

"I get sad when you don't say hello!"

He stared at Hannah for a long moment before setting the rake down, taking the cap off, and extending a weather-beaten hand. "I'm Jacob."

"You work here at the cemetery?"

"Yes, I'm a gravedigger. I'm the one who tends to all the neat graves."

"They are very neat and well kept." Hannah let her eyes wander over the old cemetery, well-kept graves, and walkways.

"I take pride in doing a good job, and cemeteries are for the living too. It's where you can find the big story. The story of the family, the lineage, the region..." Jacob suddenly became quite eloquent. "In a cemetery, history is preserved, and you must respect the dead."

"You're so right. Too many people forget where they come from, forget their history." Hannah smiled and asked, "Can I come by another time and talk to you?"

"Sure, I'm always here. I don't have much else to do."

"You're not married?"

"No, I've never had anything to do with a wife." He sighed and gripped the rake firmly. "And my only brother doesn't have time to visit me. If I call him, he doesn't bother to talk to me at all." The words suddenly came pouring out, and it was evident that it was rare for anyone to give him the time and really listen to him.

"No time..." Hannah closed her eyes and tried to think about what Virginia had taught her. She opened her eyes again and held his waning gaze. "Let me guess. When you talk to your brother, you start by complaining that it's been too long since he called you. Then you tell him that he doesn't care about you. You become self-righteous and are focused on the fact that he doesn't visit you anymore. Sound familiar?"

Jacob sighed and scraped his feet on the gravel. "Yeah, there's probably something in that."

Hannah let out an almost silent fart. "You need to forget your old ways of doing things and replace them with new ones that fit what you want."

"What do you mean?"

"You want to see your brother more often?"

"Yes, of course, he's my only family."

Hannah nodded. "When did you last ask your brother how *he* felt?"

"I can't remember."

"Then you should call him and ask how he's doing. Or better yet, go and talk to him and tell him you're sorry you don't see each other that often."

"Really?" Jacob put the rake down and stared thoughtfully at the tall girl.

"Yeah, believe me. Just try and then I'll drop by again and see how things are going."

It was a very educational trip. Hannah felt deep down that she had learned more today than she had in all the time she had been on the farm. When she tried to apply her knowledge to another person, something new and exciting happened. She suddenly realized that she could explain the same thing to many different people and get just as many different reactions.

She felt absolute joy in being able to help others. Maybe it was time to go all the way and help herself too? Maybe there was something about that sex thing. Perhaps that wasn't so bad after all...

Chapter 15

The river grew larger and more prominent at a pace that was impossible to keep up with. The great sandbank was flooded, and the river increased in strength. It was evident that it was heading for a huge waterfall.

"I'm no expert, nor do I want to be, but I like to use nature's gifts." Virginia stood in the kitchen, preparing a large bundle of beach plantain she had picked in the morning. "Today, I'll make a delicious cream stew from them."

Hannah nodded dismissively.

"It's a sustainable lifestyle when we remember to use the things right under our noses. The things that exist independently of humans. The things that have arisen because of the weather changing between sun and rain, hot and cold."

Hannah, for once, didn't listen properly; her mind was fully occupied with the thought of having sex. Ever since Virginia had visited William and talked about sex and how sex was supposed to be a wonderful experience and she suggested that Hannah find a nice guy to try to have sex with, those thoughts had been running around in her head. She was preoccupied with whether she should try touching her clitoris and start practicing, or whether it was better to find a man who would. It certainly hadn't been a nice experience to have sex with Anders. But when Virginia said that sex was supposed to be a good thing, it would probably be a good idea to try again.

"I think we need to recycle our coffee grounds; the more we can recycle, the better it is for the climate and nature." Virginia looked inquisitively at Hannah, who was still completely lost to the outside world.

A car pulled into the courtyard, and William, the fat man Hannah had seen visit Virginia a few times by then, climbed out with a little girl with red curls and many bright freckles.

"I have brought my niece with me today. We'll just buy some of your delicious seaweed chips." William looked at Virginia with admiration.

Hannah noticed Virginia straighten up and puff her chest as William looked at her. The little girl looked curiously at Virginia's long gray and black streaked hair, which for once was not pinned up with hairpins, but hanging loosely down her back.

"Are you a witch?" The girl stared at Virginia with every sign of delight. "A real live witch, like the ones in my fairy tale books?"

Virginia slapped her thigh with laughter and shook her lengthy hair so it fluttered around her ears, making her look wild and a little scary. "You have a vivid imagination, but I'm afraid I must disappoint you. I'm just an ordinary lady who lives on an old farm." To emphasize that she was perfectly ordinary, she blew a gigantic fart that reverberated in the courtyard.

The girl looked at her with every sign of delight painted on her little freckled face. "Can I light your fart on fire?"

"Yes." Virginia grinned. "A fart contains both hydrogen and methane. But please don't do that. It can be dangerous." Virginia bent down and hugged the girl, straightened up, and said softly, "Go play with the cute little kittens, my darling. I need to talk to your uncle."

Hannah stood for a moment, watching Virginia and William standing close together—as close as his fat belly would allow. She sighed in frustration and a little envy, gathered her painting stuff, and walked down to the beach.

The sun shone from a cloudless sky, and three young people were lying in the dunes. Two guys and a girl. One of the guys looked at her with interest. He was tall and handsome and nicely tanned. Hannah felt a slight stirring in her body.

Hannah set up her easel and began to paint. But she couldn't concentrate. The colors floated before her eyes, and she caught herself looking toward the young people.

The nice-looking guy caught her eye and rummaged in the pocket of his jeans for a moment before slowly walking toward her.

He cleared his throat to attract her attention. Hannah looked up, and his gaze tried to lock hers. He sent her a beaming smile.

Hannah was about to smile back when a strange thought occurred to her. There was something artificial about that smile. It almost looked as if he had been practicing it in front of a mirror. As if it was a smile he had used many times before to impress. Hannah pushed the thought away and concentrated on his clear blue eyes. His eyes were warm and easy to see through and not at all like Anders'. She had never been able to see what he was thinking.

"You haven't done much painting…" He grinned at her. "But you may have had other things in mind." He handed her a small piece of paper.

"A piece of paper from a cigarette packet?" Hannah looked at it in wonder.

"Take it." His voice was soft and seductive, and Hannah felt warmth in her chest. A warmth she hadn't felt since the time her father-in-law had hugged her.

The guy sauntered back to his friends without saying more or looking back.

Hannah looked curiously at the small piece of paper. There was a name and phone number scrawled on it.

⁓

Hannah sat up in bed and turned on the lamp on the nightstand. The little piece of paper with the guy's name and phone number was under her phone. She picked it up and looked at it. Kevin. She had never known anyone named Kevin. She liked it. She saw Kevin with her inner eye and immediately felt a pleasant warmth spread throughout her body—a heat that quickly centered around her crotch. Carefully, she placed a finger between her legs and gently touched the wet curls. It made her twitch.

She trembled and quickly moved her finger. But as intrigued as she was, something didn't feel right. No, she wasn't ready to touch herself. Perhaps she should try to call Kevin?

Deep down, she already knew she had decided to call him when she took his phone number and kept it. Perhaps she should ask Virginia for advice. Maybe she knew Kevin and knew if he was a decent guy. Hannah sighed and placed the paper with his name under her pillow. She decided to talk to Virginia in the morning and turned off the light once again.

"I don't know him very well. Just go for a walk with him, and see what happens. I have told you before that the sand pockets can be very usefull. Just use your common sense, as I have taught you, and you will always find the answer" Virginia gently pushed Hannah out the door.

"But what do you think I should do? Should I let him make love to me? You told me to find a nice man to have sex with."

Virginia didn't answer. Her mind was obviously on something else.

What was wrong with her? Hannah had never before seen Virginia like this. It had to be something serious.

Hannah called Kevin and agreed to meet him at the beach. But minutes after setting it up, she regretted it. She had a strange premonition that something terrible was going to happen. She tried to shake off the feeling as she walked down toward the beach.

"Hey, tall girl." Kevin was suddenly standing in front of her, wearing only a pair of very tight swimming trunks that left little to the imagination.

For a moment, Hannah stood uncertain with the towel wrapped around her. Then, with a small whimper, she threw it off and ran into the waves.

Kevin sat down on her towel and yelled to her from the sand, "Come up and join me!"

Hannah batted her wet hair and dove into a wave. "No, not yet. The water's really lovely." She sent Virginia a kind thought for teaching her to swim so well.

"I'm not keen on the waves." But he rose hesitantly.

"Are you coming?" Hannah asked as she rubbed water out of her eyes with both hands.

"I would love to be in the water with you, but it's much better to find a sandpit where we can be alone."

"You're scared! Are you afraid of getting wet?" Hannah teased him.

The challenge stung. "I'm not afraid!"

"Then prove it and get in the water!" She dove again and came up only a few feet from him. "You're scared," she stated.

He pondered for a few more seconds, but the bristling nipples only a few feet from him put to rest the last remnants of his fear of the waves. He reached her in three giant leaps, grabbing her in his strong arms and pressing himself against her wet body.

A huge wave came rolling in and knocked them over. Hannah quickly got to her feet and dragged a sputtering Kevin to safety on the shore.

"I guess you're not much for water." Hannah experienced a whole new feeling. A feeling that *she* was the strong one—the one in control. It was an incredible feeling, and she forgot about Kevin and why they were on the beach.

"Come with me," he pulled her up into the dunes and dumped her into an empty sand dune.

The feeling of being the strong one disappeared and now Hannah was the one who hesitated. "Are you sure we should go through with this? We don't even know each other." She was well aware that she was the one who had called Kevin, and when he had talked about wanting to have sex with her, she had said yes. After all, that was what she wanted. She desperately needed to try to forget about Anders. But But the memories of Anders and the pain associated with sex were hard to let go of.

"Lay down beside me," Kevin made room on the towel and reached for her hand.

Hannah sighed and let herself slide down onto the towel. She was kind of exited but at the same time nervous.

The wet swimsuit felt cool against her warm skin, and when Kevin gently pulled her swimsuit off, her skin was damp and cold.

"Oh my God, what happened to you?" He couldn't hold back a gasp when he saw the large scar on her left breast and the minor ones from the cigarettes Anders had pressed against her body.

"It doesn't matter. It's just something from the past." Hannah tried to recapture the feeling from the night before. The feeling of erotic desire and excitement, but she wasn't really succeeding.

Kevin mumbled: " I'm so sorry," and let his warm tongue slide down over her stomach. Her skin was smooth and golden brown except where the swimsuit had covered her, and the dark triangle between her legs turned him on. Her body was so soft and lovely. Kevin became increasingly aroused and began pulling off his swim trunks to penetrate her.

Hannah gasped, bit her lip, turned her face away, and hid it by his neck.

"Are you scared of me?" Her body lay rigid, and her face was pale and tense. "Are you not well?" he asked concerned.

"I'm okay" the answer was drawn out of her, and she could hear for herself that it didn't sound compelling.

"You don't like what I'm doing to you? Do you want me to stop?"

She shook her head. "No, I really want to try, but I've only known one other man before, and he wasn't nice to me." The night she had spent with Simon in New York had totally slipped her mind.

"Will you tell me about it?"

Hannah shook her head again. "Not now, perhaps some other time. Right now, I want you to hold me gently and take your time." She lay very still with her arms around Kevin's neck.

"I really want to make love to you. I want you to be happy." Kevin tried to be as gentle as possible.

She bravely held him close against her scarred body. She remembered clearly what would happen if she didn't make Anders happy.

Kevin felt her tremble and heard the half-quelled guttural sounds she tried to suppress. But she clung to him tenaciously.

"Make love to me. Please teach me how to enjoy it."

Hot tears spread on her face, and he hesitated only a second before his desire drove him on and, he began spreading her legs with his knees.

Hannah tried to relax but it felt all wrong. The exhilaration she'd felt the night before, lying in bed looking at the card with his phone number, was utterly gone. Somewhere, she must have known he wasn't the one. That he wasn't the Prince Charming. Not her prince, anyway. Physical satisfaction wasn't enough. It wasn't what she wanted. She wanted someone who could touch her heart.

"You're so beautiful." Kevin tried to penetrate her, but her long legs were in the way.

Hannah pushed him away and rose with a start when her keen young ear heard a strange sound.

"What the fuck are you doing here?" The girl who had been walking with the two guys on the beach the first time Hannah had seen Kevin was suddenly standing above the sand pit, looking down at them. "What the hell are you doing?"

Kevin looked embarrassed and a little silly, and Hannah thought he looked like a male cat coming home from a tiring night.

"Did you just fuck her? That tall monster girl! You are an asshole! And I've been so in love with you. You're a fucking asshole."

Kevin jumped up, grabbed his swimming trunks, and disappeared into the woods with the girl. Hannah stood back, stunned.

She sighed. It would have been so much easier if she hadn't let herself be controlled by her abdomen. Hannah stuck out her tongue in the direction of the forest where Kevin had disappeared. For a brief moment she allowed herself to think that it was all Virginia's fault, because she was always talking about sex and how important it was to learn to enjoy it. But she didn't even finish the thought before she felt bitterly ashamed. It could never be Virginia's fault.

After all, it was not Virginia but herself who had called Kevin and said she wanted to have sex with him. She was ashamed of her own weakness. What was she thinking? Blaming Virginia for something she couldn't be responsible for. It was entirely her own fault that she was now alone in a secluded sand pocket, the perfect setting for a loving couple. Suddenly the sound of running feet interrupted her thoughts and Hannah pulled on her bathing suit and stared toward the spot where the two had disappeared. She was about to give up on seeing Kevin again when he came running down toward her and jumped into the sand pit, landing right at her feet.

"Is that your girlfriend?" Hannah straightened to her full height and looked down at him.

"I'd rather be with you, " Kevin said gallantly, a little affectionately, pulling off his swimming trunks in a flash.

Hannah looked at his long slender hands. She was choking with rage and wanted more than anything to hit him.

"You must be a bigger idiot than I thought. If you imagine, I want to have sex with you now!"

"But, I'd rather have you."

"No," there was no expression in her voice or face. "We have said goodbye."

At once, there came a sharp flash of lightning and a thunderclap followed immediately. Hannah grabbed her towel and ran along the beach heading for the farm. Why had she been so stupid as to agree to be with Kevin? She would never forgive herself if anything happened to Virginia, and she had a strange feeling that something terrible was about to strike.

Chapter 16

The waters poured down without stopping, year after year, hour after hour, second after second, without stopping. At the foot of the high waterfall, pointed stones protruded from the rushing stream, and it was with life at stake that they were passed.

Leaving Kevin alone in the sand pit, Hannah ran at full speed along the beach. There was thunder and lightning, but no rain. Even at a distance, she spotted it. The light barn was on fire! For a long second that felt like a whole year, she stood frozen in terror, watching the flames break through the roof before she set off running along the shore. If only she'd had her phone with her, she could have called for help.

The old wooden staircase leading up from the beach shook and rocked as Hannah leaped like a gazelle— three steps at a time.

The scalding yellow glow from the burning barn was so bright it almost blinded her, and she ran for the old door.

"Damn it!" Hannah sobbed. The door was locked from the inside. She lunged and kicked wildly with her strong right leg, hoping to get the door open. She knew in her heart that Virginia was still there, knew that she had not managed to get out of the burning building. She heard Virginia's call as clearly as if she were standing next to her. *Come, my sweet girl, hurry... I'm waiting for you...*

The flames rode merrily on the west wind, roaring in red and gold, spreading across the thatched roof and now taking hold of the main house. She could feel the heat coming in mighty blasts, curling up all the greenery around her. Suddenly a gust of wind sent a bank of black smoke over her, making her cough and her eyes burn and water.

In the cloud of smoke, there was a smell, a smell of burning flesh.

Hannah straightened up and gave the door another kick; this time, she managed to open it. Without thinking, she banged her head against the door frame and rushed into the burning building. The heat was so intense that she involuntarily stepped backward before dropping to her knees and quickly crawling further into the burning barn.

She knew deep in her heart that it was too late. She also knew where to find Virginia. Her favorite place. The vast built-in sofa at the big brass lamp. Hannah crawled purposefully forward, allowing no other thought but this one—I've got to get Virginia out of here.

The heat ached in her face. She reached the sofa, which was engulfed in flames. She tried desperately to find Virginia and suddenly she felt an arm. She grabbed Virginia's arm from the flames and pulled with all her might.

As if the flames knew their prey was helpless, they rushed forward eagerly and triumphantly, devouring everything in their path.

Hannah pulled once more, bringing Virginia's limp body to the floor. There was no time to think; it had to be quick. She took a firm grip on her ankles and began to pull her across the floor towards the life-giving air. She forced herself against the heat to reach the door, but it was almost palpable, a barrier of red flickering firelight.

She could feel the heat making the skin on her face swell and tighten.

Virginia tried to speak but couldn't make a single sound. Her hair was burnt, and her cheeks and chin had burn marks all over them. The black-crusted mask had patches of bare flesh, and a large blister that looked like a giant bright grape was on her cheek.

Hannah screamed and wanted to back away and run to safety but forced herself to grip Virginia's ankles tighter in a last-ditch effort to drag her to safety. Hannah knew in her heart that Virginia was dying. No human could survive such terrible burns.

"Help will be here soon," Hannah whispered, tears running down her cheeks.

Virginia slowly opened her eyes. "Thank God," she murmured. "I wanted you here. I waited for you to come." Her voice was almost inaudible. "Promise me you'll continue what you and I have discussed. It's the right path for you."

"But I can't do it alone. I can't do it without your help, it's impossible." Hannah was crying openly now, trying to visualize how far she was from the door and the safety outside.

"Promise," Virginia demanded. There was something terribly urgent in her words. "Promise me. Don't doubt yourself." The last words were almost impossible to decipher, and Virginia's chest stopped moving. Her body suddenly went limp.

Hannah threw herself over Virginia's limp body, squeezed her hands, and cried: "No, no."

A voice from outside reached through the roar of the flames. Hannah realized she was very close to the door now. A brown stain appeared on one of her arms, and her blouse began to burn. Hannah screamed in anguish and pain, an eerie sound that dissipated through the roar and crackle of the flames. But the fear and pain were the key that unlocked her last power resources.

As if Virginia had been a rag doll, she pulled her out through the door, where a pair of strong hands grabbed her. Through a haze of pain, she heard the ambulance coming, and just before she fainted, she saw Virginia's limp body being carefully placed on a gurney.

On the morning after the fire, when the first pearly glow of daylight was visible on the eastern horizon, the remains of the farm could be clearly seen - the sad remains of the Farm on The Edge of The World. Two of the three wings had burned out, and the roof was gone; only the walls remained. Everything that survived was sooty, and an unpleasant, impenetrable smell of smoke and burnt flesh hung in the air. Not a single bird chirped, and not a single wind blew. The whole area around the farm seemed lifeless. It was deathly quiet.

The elderly man from the neighboring farm who had scolded Virginia for letting Hannah move in, stood in the woods, looking at the farm. "Alas, no that it should end like this." A tear ran down his cheek. "The sins of the past—one can never be free of them." He wiped the tear from his cheek and slowly turned his back to the burnt farm.

Chapter 17

The vast, violent waterfall threw its masses of water into the depths, reluctantly letting go of what was carried along. But the momentum was too strong, and the water masses had to follow the current.

Hannah felt like she was flying, like she was in the sky, looking down at the winding river deep below her. The greater the joy, the greater the pain that followed. Hannah was dreaming, a nightmare where she could smell burnt flesh and fear swept through her. Her skin was melting.

History repeated itself, but this time, it wasn't a gentle and loving female voice that brought her back to life. This time, a deep, warm, fatherly voice entered her tortured brain, drawing her out of the gray fog of fear that had overtaken her.

When Hannah woke, she found herself in a strange bed wearing hospital clothes, and there wasn't a place on her tall body that didn't hurt. But even the intense pain couldn't drown out her internal ache, the pain she felt now that she was once again alone. Her rudder was gone, gone forever. Hannah gently tried to wiggle her toes and realized that for once, they were resting on the mattress. She was in a bed long enough for her tall body!

"Where am I?" Hannah's voice was as faint as gentle spring rain on a windowpane.

"At the hospital." The deep voice seemed soothing and made her body relax.

"Where?" Hannah repeated.

"You were flown by helicopter to Copenhagen. Here we can give you the best care."

"Care?" Hannah felt herself slipping into darkness again.

"You have second-degree burns in several places on your body and are severely weakened."

Hannah fell over the waterfall, and the dream of the river began again. The river had no end. She was tossed about in the waves and crashed against the large rocks that jutted up, only to be immediately washed away. On down the river that never stopped.

Hannah woke again and once again, didn't know where she was. It was dark and quiet around her. She lay briefly, trying to collect her thoughts, and suddenly everything became clear. She tried to sit up in bed but had to give in. The light was turned on, and a nurse entered the room.

"At last, you are awake. That's good." The nurse quickly checked that the connected tubes and equipment were working and tucked the duvet better around Hannah's tall body. "You've been fortunate. Your burns are not as bad as we feared at first, and miraculously, there are no signs of smoke inhalation. We'll keep you for a week or two until you fully recover, and then you can go home."

Home... where was home now? Once again, she had no home and no future. All joy had vanished from Hannah's life. Her entire existence felt like a void, causing chronic pain. The pain could be so intense, like a violent cramp, that it made her cringe. She felt an emptiness and meaninglessness everywhere. It was an effort just to keep her eyes open. She closed her eyes and fell asleep once more.

When Hannah opened her eyes again, a man stood beside her bed, a tall man, a very tall man—in a white jacket. When he spoke, she immediately realized that it was his soft, warm voice that had brought her back to life.

Hannah turned her head a bit and looked at him with a slightly surprised expression. He was a nice-looking man, with dark brown hair that was gray at the temples, big hands, and a powerful build but not fat. Hannah wiggled one foot gently and looked at the doctor. "The bed is long enough for me. My feet don't stick out at all."

The doctor smiled, and it was a nice smile, a friendly smile, a smile that made Hannah feel a faint shiver, a faint feeling that maybe one day everything would be less challenging, perhaps even good again.

"We do everything for our patients here at the hospital. Of course, we have extra-long beds for our very special patients!" He made it sound like she was a very important person. "You just need to rest and relax. There's nothing wrong with you, but time and rest can cure. By the way, my name is Dr. Dahl, but you can call me Adam. We're not very formal here. And by the way, I'm the head doctor here in the department." He took her hand, and she felt the warmth of the large hand fill her as she dozed off again.

Hannah dreamed of hairpins. The long, U-shaped hairpins that were constantly slipping out of Virginia's hair and lying everywhere. The hairpin she had brought to New York and had lost there. All the hairpins she'd picked up and put in the bowl on the coffee table. In Hannah's confused mind, the hairpins became a monster trying to hold her down.

Hannah woke up from her nightmare and cried silently. If only she'd had one of those long black hairpins, she would have had a physical reminder of the woman she loved more than life itself. She dozed off again, the unpleasant dream continued, and fear passed through her.

"Wake up, you're dreaming again..."

Through the gray fog of fear, she recognized the soft, warm voice—the tall man with the gentle eyes and nice smile. He stood at the window, staring at the dark clouds.

"You're here again. Don't you ever work?" Hannah would have thought that a senior doctor in a large hospital was always busy.

"I do work." Adam smiled at her.

"What about your patients?"

"I'm with one of them." He turned toward the bed as if an invisible thread was pulling at him.

Hannah blinked, trying to let go of her nightmare as a strange sense of security spread through her. There was something about that man that made her feel safe. His warm hand on her forehead made her open her eyes fully.

"Virginia?" The unspoken question was finally asked.

Adam looked at her with the most profound compassion in his gray eyes. "She didn't survive the fire. The funeral has taken place in silence. I am sorry for your loss. But all you have to do now is focus on getting better." He bent over her, and for a moment, Hannah thought he was going to reach out and stroke her hair. But he slowly took his hand away without touching her.

She was surprised to see Adam staring at her. It was as if he was unable to take his eyes off her. Hannah closed her eyes again. It was too much to think about. Virginia was dead, and Hannah herself was alive and once again alone without a home.

"Why? Why Virginia? She had so much to live for. It would have been much better if it had been me," Hannah muttered, her eyes still closed.

"Stop!" Adam took her hand and squeezed it so hard she opened her eyes. "Don't you start thinking about that!"

"What?"

"That it's your fault. That it should have been you instead."

Her sobs filled the room, and her closed eyes overflowed with tears, but Adam's warm hand against her forehead made her doze off.

When she woke again, it was evening, and the tubes she'd been hooked up to had been removed, leaving her feeling an indefinable sense of freedom.

Adam opened the door to the hospital room and gave her a big smile. He was still wearing his medical gown, but it was unbuttoned, and he looked more relaxed than earlier in the day.

"Can you get up and go to the bathroom yourself?"

"I think so." She gently flipped the duvet aside and sat tentatively on the edge of the bed. Her long legs tried to gain support on the floor, but she couldn't find her footing and wobbled, and everything spun around.

"Let me help you." Adam was suddenly at her side and gently helped her to her feet. A faint hiss of air leaving her bowels made him smile.

"Shit," she muttered, squeezing her buttocks together. She suddenly realized that he was a little taller than her, because she had to crane her neck back a little to look him in the eye.

"Call me if you need help." Adam led her into the bathroom and placed her on the seat before closing the door.

"How do you feel now?" Adam watched her as she lay back in bed. He tried to read her body language. "Are you sorry you couldn't be there for the funeral?"

Hannah shook her head. "There must be something wrong with me. I don't feel anything anymore. It was only at first that I felt everything was hopeless. Now I feel nothing. Absolutely nothing."

"That's perfectly normal. You have to take care of yourself, and the only way your brain can deal with the situation is by suppressing your emotions."

"I feel like I'm a terrible person." Hannah began to cry. "I loved Virginia more than I've ever loved anyone. She was everything to me, yet I can't grieve anymore."

"That's perfectly normal," Adam repeated. "You're going to grieve later. When you're ready, it'll all come back to you, and then you'll have to face your feelings and get them out of your system. You're just not ready for that yet, so that's why there's no way out but to suppress them. Don't be so hard on yourself."

Hannah felt the tears welling up.

"You'll need time to get over it. A long time. Maybe many, many years. But that doesn't mean you can't live in the meantime. There's no sensible reason you should die too and let your life be over. Not physically over, but psychologically. You are allowed to live and get well again."

"Are you serious?"

"Yes, of course. I didn't know Virginia, but from what you've told me about her, I'm convinced she would want you to move on with your life. Isn't that right?"

Hannah nodded. "Yes, she certainly would. She was so selfless. She always wanted what was best for everyone else."

"There, you see? Now let the past rest for a while, and when you're ready to take on the challenge of getting it processed and closed, just open back up and get it done. But until then, remember to live!"

Adam stroked her hair before leaving the room, leaving Hannah to think about what he had said.

Hannah slept, and in her sleep, her emotions ran free. In her sleep, she could grieve for Virginia. In her dreams, she relived the nightmare when the farm burned, and she couldn't save the person she loved more than life itself. She twisted and turned and whimpered. But suddenly, the dream changed, and a deep, masculine voice once again penetrated her depressed state of mind, and her dream changed. The nightmare was over, giving way to a new set of emotions.

In the dream, she asked herself, "Why aren't you afraid of those feelings?" The answer came to her immediately: "I'm terrified, but I can't let the memories of Anders rule my life." She dreamed on and heard a voice say, "Mature men will pursue you, and young men will be afraid of you!"

When she opened her eyes several hours later, Adam stood beside her bed. He watched her intently and smiled when he saw her gaze light up when she realized he was there.

She hesitated, then said, "I dreamed of you."

"About me?" Adam looked at her teasingly. "And may I ask what you were dreaming about?"

"No," she blushed. "I can't tell you that."

"Why not? I am a doctor, so I can handle it."

The dream frightened her into discovering that she had feelings for him. Feelings she had sworn not to feel again after the years with Anders. Neither Simon nor Kevin had meant anything to her. The night with Simon had been her only option at the time, and Kevin had been her stupid and immature attempt to find a sexual partner. There hadn't been a single real emotion involved. But Adam meant something else to her. There was definitely emotion involved and it scared her.

"What did I say?" He was still smiling.

"You didn't say anything."

"Did I do anything?"

She blushed even more, and the pink color spread down her long, beautiful neck.

"What did I do?" He repeated the question to give her time to compose herself.

"I can't tell you that." Hannah closed her eyes tightly and pretended to fall asleep.

"You're so beautiful," Adam said suddenly, as if pulling the words out of the air.

Hannah opened her eyes and looked at him in surprise.

"Your hair looks so pretty in the glare of the setting sun." He stood by the window but didn't let her out of sight.

As she drank her juice, they kept looking straight into each other's eyes, and she felt a slight tingle in her stomach.

Suddenly, she found herself thinking about how it would feel to be kissed by him, how it would feel to have his big hands on her body. Adam patted her gently on the cheek and said, "Sleep now. I'll check on you again very soon." He released her gaze and walked toward the door. "I must leave you to check on the other patients for a while, but I'll be back."

Long after he had left, she lay with her eyes closed, imagining what it would be like to be naked and make love to him. Until, with a little cry, she opened her eyes and tried to banish the image from her mind. He was only her doctor, for God's sake. She would never see him again once she was discharged from the hospital.

⁓

"Please sit down," Hannah said, pointing to the chair next to the bed. Adam sat down awkwardly, and Hannah noticed that his cheeks were red. "I don't know how to thank you for everything you've done for me. Thanks to you, I didn't break down completely after the accident. Because of you, I'm starting to feel like life is worth living again."

Adam's hand closed around hers, squeezing it tightly, but he said nothing. They sat looking at each other for a long time until

Adam finally broke the silence. "I don't know if I've ever known someone well enough to understand them, me included. But I do know that I want to know you—know you better and in a different way than I do now as my patient."

"I didn't know that," Hannah murmured.

"You must have noticed," Adam said, the shadow of a smile sliding across his face.

"Well, I wasn't entirely honest. I know you want to get to know me better," she replied.

Adam released her hand but continued to hold her gaze. Hannah sighed and stretched, making all her joints creak.

"My whole body feels like I've been sleeping in the same position for nineteen years."

"Do you want a massage?" Adam looked at her left foot sticking out from under the duvet. "What about a nice foot massage? I'm afraid the rest of your body can't handle being massaged just yet." He looked at her with an expression of the deepest pity.

"Yes, that would be lovely." Hannah assumed he would call a physical therapist. But instead, he threw the covers aside and knocked the headboard down so she lay flat on the bed.

Adam pulled the duvet away and cupped her feet in his warm hands.

She sighed and relaxed and Adam started gently rubbing her feet. "Oh, it feels wonderful..."

He kept on massaging and looked into her eyes. He said nothing, but she could clearly read in his eyes that he desired her, that he thought of her as something other than a patient. His eyes changed expression, and there was a curious gleam in them that Hannah couldn't decipher.

He stood up slowly. "I have to leave you now." He left her without looking back.

But even long after he was gone, Hannah could see the look of desire in his eyes and feel a warm sensual tension between her legs. She lay still, enjoying the feeling, before falling into a deep sleep and beginning to dream. A good dream this time. A dream where she was floating in a warm current of happiness. A dream she didn't want to wake up from.

Hannah admitted to herself that she looked all right now as she viewed her body in the mirror of the hospital's small bathroom one morning two weeks after the fire. Her body was almost completely healed. Of course, there were still scars in several places on her body, new ones next to the scars she had already had for a long time, but they didn't hurt anymore, and only time could make them prettier. It wasn't the scars on her body that bothered her either. It mattered little to her how she looked.

What mattered was how she felt. The very thought of going home to some new unknown place and being all alone again frightened her. It scared her beyond belief, she admitted to herself with some difficulty. Where would she go? Her mother was not an option; she was in Thailand with her latest boyfriend. Her father was busier than usual and probably had a new lady on the go too. Neither of them had visited her in the hospital. She was nearly twenty and as an adult, could decide for herself.

A nurse came into her room and smiled at her. "How are you today? You look well."

Hannah looked back at the nurse and tried to smile, but it stuck on her lips.

The experienced nurse looked at her inquiringly. "Hmm, not doing so well today, I guess. I'll see if I can get Dr. Dahl to drop by later."

"I hear you've had a bad day," Adam said quietly, having found time to drop by her room several hours later. The last five days, she hadn't seen him much. It was as if he'd stayed away on purpose.

"Yeah, I don't know why. I can't find myself at all, and there's nothing I want to do. It's all just gray and unimportant." She watched his gray-streaked hair fall into his eyes every time he bowed. "You need a haircut," she said only half-jokingly.

He smiled. "Yes, you're right, but I haven't had time. Hairdressers aren't open at night, so I rarely get it done."

"I can give you a haircut," she offered, regretting it the second the words left her lips.

"Can you cut my hair?" He grinned and winked at her. "That's a fantastic offer! I'd be a fool not to take you up on it." He regarded her inquiringly. "If you really mean you'll cut my hair, we should make a deal."

Hannah mostly wanted to say it was said in jest, but then she looked at him again, and he held her gaze with his warm gray eyes. They were kind eyes. He was an incredibly nice man. Why not just cut his hair? She knew she could easily do it, even though it had been a while since she'd last used scissors.

When she cut Anders' hair, he had always made her feel useless and stupid. But she knew in her heart that this man, this mature doctor, would never do anything to make her feel that way. He would always act like a gentleman and make her feel good.

"Yes, I meant what I said," she replied quietly. "I want to cut your hair. But when and where, and how do I get a pair of scissors and a good comb?"

"Let me see." He checked on his phone. "How about tomorrow afternoon, we'll go out together and buy what you need. Then we'll drive to my place, and you can cut my hair. Then I'll drive you back here when we're ready. What do you say to that plan? I will change it to an open admission, and then there is no problem with you leaving the hospital."

Hannah moistened her lips and checked inside. Was going out with her doctor the right thing for her to do? She breathed deeply a few times and closed her eyes, contemplating. Yes, it felt right. "That sounds like an excellent plan," she replied slowly. "I'd like that." But suddenly she remembered something. "I have no clothes. All my belongings are burnt."

"Just leave it to me. I have an idea." Adam left the room, leaving Hannah with a questioning look on her face.

Later in the afternoon, a visitor came by and she almost fell out of bed in surprise. Her *mother* had come to visit.

"I got a call from an angry man who said he was the head doctor here, and he ordered me to buy you some clothes. He ordered me! He didn't even think of the fact that I had a thousand other things to do." Her mother placed a large shopping bag at the floor and only now did she glance at her daughter. "When you're lying down, it's hard to see how tall you really are…"

Hannah sighed, but remembered what Virginia had taught her about always answering politely. "Thank you, Mom. It was really nice of you to bring me some clothes."

"What does he look like, the head doctor? Is he a handsome guy?" Her mother got a twinkle in her eye that Hannah remembered only too well.

"He's far too old for you." Hannah smiled inwardly as she watched her mother slump a little, and after standing uncertainly looking out the window for a minute or so, she disappeared again without saying goodbye.

Hannah opened the bag curiously. It contained some underwear, a blouse and skirt, and a pair of black boots. She wondered if her mother had chosen the clothes or if Adam had told her what to buy.

~~~

"Can I do what I could before the accident?" Hannah had dressed and was waiting for him when he entered the room.

He looked at her appraisingly, letting his gaze slide slowly from the top of her wild brown hair to her half-high black boots.

"You can do exactly what you did before the accident. There is nothing physically wrong with you. You just need time to remedy the rest. Your scars will get better with time—less red and not nearly as visible. But nothing has changed."

"Well, I feel different now." She didn't dare meet his appraising gaze.

"Different in what way?"

"I was insecure when I came to The Farm on The Edge of The World. And for the barely two years I lived there with Virginia, I felt security, a certainty that everything would be all right. Not just good, but amazing. And now, I don't know what to feel. After a short period, when things are going really well, the pain comes back with renewed force. I'm not sure if I dare live again. Whether I dare feel good again because I know it won't last. That there will be another period of pain. That somehow it's *my* fault that so much pain comes when I love someone."

He looked at her intently. "Your rational mind knows that's not right. That's not how things work, but I understand why you're having trouble letting reason prevail for now. Why not just try to let it go for a while? It's not something you need to worry about right now, is it? Right now, you and I are just going shopping, and then you'll cut my hair so I can look my patients in their eyes again." His smile warmed her to the core. "Come on." He extended his warm hand toward her. "My car is just down here, so let's get going and see what we can get."

Once they were in the car, Hannah turned to Adam and began watching him closely.

"I get all embarrassed when you look at me in that judgmental way," he grinned, steering the car carefully through rush hour traffic.

She just smiled and continued to look at him.

"I'm not used to a pretty young girl looking at me like that. I'm just boring old me!"

"How old are you then?"

"Forty-seven." He didn't bat an eye at her.

Hannah smiled at him. He looked younger. A very tall and handsome man. Light brown hair that was turning gray at the sides. Gray eyes and powerfully built without being fat. He looked like he was rarely outdoors, but he was probably working all the time and didn't get out much.

"You've never been married?" It wasn't the question she had planned to ask him, but it slipped out.

"Yes," Adam nodded and took her hand. "Once, about ten years ago. We were only married for a scant year—we were very different. She wanted to marry a doctor and have a secure life where she didn't have to work. But when she realized that I had to work a lot to earn money for the house, cars, and vacations, she got bored and quickly found another man who was much more exciting than me." He tightened his grip on her hand and continued. "Medicine is never boring, and it is my life. Until now, medicine has been my whole life, but I hope that will change soon." He looked at her but didn't elaborate on what he meant.

Hannah smoothed down her clothes, suddenly feeling happy and lighthearted, knowing she looked better than she had in weeks. The yellow blouse with many little silver buttons, black skirt, and boots made her feel beautiful.

Suddenly, as he stopped at a red light, he leaned forward and kissed her on the mouth. Hannah gasped in surprise. "I like you; I like you a lot, and I think you know it," he explained.

"And when you like a girl, you kiss her?" Hannah suddenly realized that she was flirting with him.

"I haven't kissed a girl in so long that I can't remember the last time. I'm not typically the kind of guy who kisses my patients; I want you to know that."

She looked at him with tenderness in her eyes. "I understand. You don't have to explain; I'm aware that you're a reliable person. That's why I like you."

"Ah," he said teasingly, "you like me?"

"Yes, isn't it obvious? I returned your kiss, even though it's been a long time since I've kissed someone." She remembered the last time clearly but pushed the thought away immediately. She certainly didn't want to start thinking about that again. All sorts of accidents had happened the last time she kissed a man. She needed to try kissing again and see what happened.

At the next red light, Adam kissed her again, and Hannah sighed deeply with contentment.

He parked the car in an empty space well away from the entrance to the department store. Before she could open the door, he slipped around the car and opened it.

"May I offer you my arm? Right now, you are not my patient. You are just a beautiful woman spending an evening in town with a boring elderly man," he grinned.

"What about when we get back to the hospital. Will I just be your patient again?" Her eyes promised him yet undiscovered pleasures if he answered the innocent question correctly.

"No." His voice was calm and firm. "No, you are so much more than just my patient. I don't want to move too fast but rather take things slowly; it suits my nature best. I don't know what's happening to me, but I'm acting like a crazy teenager when I'm near you. I've never experienced that before. But you can be quite sure you are something special, and I will tell you more when you are ready to hear it. But come on." He took her hand and helped her out of the car. "First, we're going to buy some scissors and whatever else you need, and then you're going to show me what you are capable of."

"Wait," she murmured, following willingly as he walked to the entrance. "You just wait; I'll show you what I'm made of."

∕̇2̇

"That looks really smart." Adam stood in front of the mirror in the hallway, admiring his new hairstyle. "I've got to show off my new hair! Would you do me the great pleasure of going out to dinner with me?"

Hannah nodded. She could still feel the sensation of his back against her stomach and abdomen as she stood behind him and cut his overly long hair.

"Great, then let's find a good place where we can eat and dance." Adam suddenly realized that his need to have a legitimate reason to hold her in his arms had to be satisfied.

They stood close together as they rode the elevator down into the parking garage to his big black Audi. It was an incredibly sensual experience riding in that car, like nothing she had ever experienced before. She naturally feared cars after her time with

Anders and the accident, but the luxury car Adam drove evoked no unpleasant memories. Hannah looked at him with a gentle smile on her face. Adam drove the car with both hands on the steering wheel and obeyed the speed limit. She relaxed and got more comfortable in the seat. It was nice to have a man she could trust. And she knew in her heart that Adam would never do anything to hurt her. "Do you realize this is the first time a man has asked me out to dinner?"

"No, I thought you've had many other admirers." Adam looked at her, puzzled.

"You don't know anything about me." Hannah sighed deeply and studied Adam's hands lying calmly on the white tablecloth. Long, strong hands. Hands that would never hurt her. Never lay hands on her and force her to do something that hurt or something she didn't agree with. She sighed again and looked him straight in the eyes. "Before I moved to the farm and Virginia, I lived with a man for almost two years." She hesitated, but forced herself to continue. "You've seen the scars on my body. The old scars from all the times Anders pressed a burning cigarette against my skin."

Adam reached for her hand and kissed it. "Where were your parents in all this?"

"They were never present, or if present, didn't care about me. I never felt like I had any parents."

"Didn't care?" Adam was deeply shocked.

Hannah didn't answer but looked at her plate, where the fresh green asparagus suddenly made her remember the delicious seaweed she had so often collected and then eaten during her time on the farm. A tear ran down her cheek and Adam gently wiped it away with his warm hand.

"You don't have to tell me more. I understand that you haven't had the happy childhood and youth I had hoped for. I can't do anything about your past, but if you will let me, I will do my best to make your future as bright and easy as possible."

Hannah nodded and concentrated on the food on her plate, but she had no idea of what she was eating. He wanted to take care of her. The last time a man had said that to her, it had gone horribly wrong. Did she dare to try again?

"Wanna dance?" Adam asked the second they finished dessert.

Hannah took his hand and was about to follow him onto the dance floor when a nearby voice stopped her.

"How can a girl be so tall? That's not normal. There must be something wrong with you." A woman in a big, flowered dress and a lot of gold jewelry stared unabashedly at Hannah.

"That's no way to address a beautiful woman!" Adam sent the lady an angry look.

Hannah laughed. "I'm used to it. As a tall woman, one must be able to tolerate a little of everything. I didn't like it when I was a child and a teenager, but now I'm proud of my height. People often stare at me like I'm a celebrity, and I'm starting to appreciate it."

She could feel Adam's hand against her back as they danced, and he had pulled her so close to him that her breasts pressed against him, and his legs rubbed up against hers as they twirled in the restaurant's dim lighting.

"Come, let's go." Adam led her out toward the car.

She stopped in front of him. She had to kiss him. Needed to feel his lips against hers. She put her arms around his neck. It was so nice being with a man she didn't have to bend her neck to kiss.

Adam gasped for breath, feeling as if he had just run a marathon, and Hannah slid her fingers caressingly over his neck and pressed her body against his. The air around her filled with her scent. Adam looked at her with a gentle and loving expression on his mature face. "You told me a few days ago that you had dreamt about me. Do you remember?"

"Yes…" She didn't dare meet his gaze.

"Now will you tell me what you dreamed?" He took her hand.

"You had taken off your clothes." Hannah looked at the ground, embarrassed.

"All my clothes?"

She nodded. "Yes, you were completely naked."

"And?"

"I could tell you needed me. That you would never hurt me. That you meant it when you said you cared for me and wanted to be with me. I could feel your kindness and love, and if you still wanted to, I'd go home with you." The last words came so softly that he could hardly hear them.

He kissed her hard and pulled her close.

She let out a gasp as she felt him, and a thrill ran through her body. For a long time, she stayed like that, her hips pressed against his and her breasts pressed flat against his jacket.

He forgot everything about going slow as his hands began to move up her hard, taut back, his mouth forcing hers up so that her soft lips parted like the fleshy red petals of a classic fragrant rose in full bloom.

She could clearly feel that he was aroused, but when he moved a little and pressed his bulge even harder against her abdomen, the sound in her throat turned into a panicked, protesting moan and she tried to wriggle out of his arms.

He let go of her abruptly when he saw the frightened look in her eyes. "This won't do." He sighed. "I'm taking you back to the hospital now."

Chapter 18

The river widened and became a tranquil stream with large flat stones and soft sandbanks. The flat rocks and shallow, calm water made navigation wonderfully easy.

Hannah lay on the bed, staring at the ceiling. It was three days since she had seen Adam. The strength of the missing surprised her. Something had happened to her in the short time she had known him. She had begun to feel something she had never felt in nearly twenty years. Why didn't he come, though? Didn't he understand that she needed him?

She called the nurse. "Where's Adam? I'm not feeling very well today."

"You look well." The nurse smiled at Hannah. In the two weeks Hannah had been in the hospital, a tremendous change had happened to her. Especially in the last few days, she had blossomed like a rose that had stood in an empty vase and had finally been watered and regained her freshness and beauty.

"He's busy, but I will tell him you want him to visit. By the way, he told me this morning that you can go home very soon. There is nothing more we can do for you here."

Hannah just stood there. Why didn't Adam come? Was he really just going to avoid her? The nurse, who had since walked out, popped her head back in and said that Adam would come by later to see her.

A few hours later, he finally walked in. He looked tired and distracted. Hannah ran to him and let her hand slide over his neat, short hair. She could still feel the sensation of his back against her body as she cut his hair. "I have missed you. Don't you think it would be nice if you kissed me hello?"

A startled expression slid across his face before he gently kissed her on the cheek and promptly pulled back. "You're scaring me." Adam took another step back without taking his eyes off her.

"You scare me too." Hannah was being honest. Part of her wanted so badly to make love to Adam, but the memories of Anders, Simon, and Kevin wouldn't disappear.

"I'm scared shitless. But I hate being scared." With that, Adam took a step toward her.

"I'd better..." Hannah hesitated, took a calming breath, but only managed to gasp. "I shouldn't..." She was about to say some more but stopped when Adam took a gentle hold of her arm.

"Time to go for a drive," he said.

∕ℓ—

Hannah sat on the rooftop terrace of Adam's apartment, looking across the peaceful canal. Just then, Adam walked out with a bottle of wine in his hand.

Hannah tried to be bold and confident and not let the inner turmoil sweep over her. "You would have slept with me if you could handle making love to someone like me. Since you stopped and drove me home last time, you obviously couldn't." She felt an illogical urge to hurt him by being rude. An urge sprung from the defense mechanism she had developed almost to perfection over the years.

Adam stopped abruptly as if he had bumped into a glass wall. "What the hell do you mean by that? Someone like you—I get angry when I hear you say things like that." He moved quickly and was about to grab her arm when she took flight and slipped between the couch and the window.

Her attempt to escape was a simple reflex reaction. She was only afraid of her own emotions. She wasn't even sure she could handle *feeling* anything. And she already knew that Adam wasn't just a man she could have casual sex with once or twice. He already meant more to her.

"I wanted to be with you that night when we'd gone out to dinner, but I wanted it a little too much ... for my own good and yours. I've been walking with the taste of you inside me ever since, and the way I see it now, there's only one way we can work all this out. I want you."

"Want what?"

"You! All of you!"

Something fell into place inside her. Blood rushed to her cheeks but just as quickly disappeared again. "You can't just say something like that. You can't just expect..."

"I'm not counting on anything, and I'm not just saying anything. I won't waste any more words. I just want to hold you. I want to kiss you on the neck and let my lips slide down the lovely curves of your neck. You are such a beautiful woman."

"Am I beautiful?" Hannah suddenly felt a strong desire to hear him say it again.

"Yes, you are beautiful, and I want you so much, I can't wait any longer."

Hannah opened her eyes wide and saw the desire in his eyes. But she also saw something else. She saw emotions—genuine emotions—emotions that matched the ones she felt herself, and she pressed herself against him with an impetuosity neither of them had expected.

"May I?" he asked.

"No, you may not." She barely had time to see the light go out in his eyes as she pulled him down against her. "You may not, but you *must*."

Adam pressed his lips to hers, kissing her hard without the warmth and gentleness he'd otherwise shown her before. He pressed his body relentlessly against hers as if his pounding heart was beating directly against her. He swept her up in his arms and carried her off the terrace, into the apartment, and into the bedroom.

He gently laid her down on the snow-white bedspread. "You are so beautiful!"

Hannah saw his emotions reflected in his eyes. He thought she was beautiful. She could see that clearly. It wasn't just something he said. He meant it.

"So are you. You look really handsome with your new hair," Hannah teased him, unbuttoning her blouse. Her firm young breasts with rosy nipples came into view. The scars from the burning cigarettes were pink against her white skin. But the newly healed burns showed even more clearly. His eyes darkened with compassion as he gasped for breath and began to unzip his pants. It had to be done quickly. He couldn't wait. Everything in him was screaming to possess the lovely young girl lying half naked and willing on his bed.

He gently lay down next to her and was about to take her in his arms and kiss her.

"Why do you stop?"

He muttered something she couldn't hear.

"Don't you want me?"

"Yes." He was red in the face. "Yes, of course I do, but I have to stop now."

"Why?" She didn't understand a word of it.

"I have to fart ... right now..." He tried to roll off, but she held him tight.

"Please fart; it doesn't scare me. Virginia taught me that a fart must never be taboo. It's a natural part of life. As Virginia always said, *let the wind and weather take its course.*" Hannah teased him, "And you're a doctor. You must know it's perfectly natural to fart. It's just hot air. It doesn't mean anything. You may fart all you want."

"You really mean that?" Adam tried to make the fart as silent as possible but couldn't help a good pop escape.

She slapped him gently on the buttocks. "Are there more farts on the way? Then I think you should press them out before we continue what we're here for."

She had never thought a relationship could be like this. For the first time ever, she was beginning to feel safe with a man. Hannah discovered she enjoyed his kisses and the feeling of his hand caressing her breast. Many of the old unresolved feelings surfaced, and tears came to her eyes.

Adam gently wiped them away, and when he pulled off her panties and let his warm hand slide down between her legs, she didn't stop him. She wanted to feel his kisses on her neck, on her breasts, and wanted to feel his body against hers.

After their first extraordinary lovemaking session, Adam held her close against his warm body. "I know we haven't known each other intimately for more than a few hours, but I hope you'll consider moving in with me."

Hannah gasped, and a little warm air escaped between her buttocks. "Live here with you? I certainly seemed to have heard this particular chief doctor say that he liked to do things slowly and at a steady pace."

Adam nodded. "It used to be so, but all I can think about right now is you and how wonderful it will be for us to be together. And you're ready to be discharged. I can discharge you as early as tomorrow morning. You don't need to stay in the hospital."

"I feel safe with you." Hannah snuggled better in his arms.

"Then tell me you want to move in with me. Please?"

"That's probably the best offer I'll get." She laughed, and when her bottom immediately let loose a little fart, she said, "It certainly sounds as if my bottom already feels at home here with you!"

～

"Why do I have to be blindfolded?" Hannah laughed. "What are you up to?"

Adam didn't answer but tied the wide silk ribbon across her eyes. "Come on, we're going out on the terrace."

Gently, he led her through the door and to the glass screen. He turned her around so her back was to the glass and carefully removed the silk ribbon from her face.

"Will you marry me?" Adam knelt on the roof terrace in front of her.

"Marry?" Hannah gasped in surprise. She hadn't seen that coming. After all, they had only known each other for such a short time. Four weeks to be precise. She looked at the terrace floor in amazement. He had strewn rose petals and set out a small table with pink champagne, two glasses, and an enormous bouquet of red roses.

"I love you; you must know that." Adam didn't take his eyes off her. "I love you so much that the only right thing is for us to get married. But of course..." He suddenly thought of something, and his face darkened. "If you don't love me..."

Hannah's feelings for the tall, sweet, kind doctor were the strongest she had felt since Virginia had lived. She nodded slowly. "Yes, I love you." Adam's face brightened. "I love you very much, and yes, I will marry you." She had no time to say more before he had enveloped her in his strong arms and kissed her so fiercely that they both forgot time and place.

Hannah came to her senses first. "Don't you think we'd better go inside? What comes next is nobody's business but our own."

Adam grinned. "Yes, you're right. A rooftop in the middle of Copenhagen isn't the right place for what I'm about to do to you."

She didn't realize that she was using sex to forget the horrors of the past, but whenever the thoughts of Virginia became too much to bear and tried to penetrate her armor, she would engage in new activities with Adam; activities that almost always involved sexual release. Every orgasm that Adam gave her made her repress the past even more and thereby feel a little better. It was a similar feeling to the old days when she threw up and briefly felt better afterwards.

⁓

They wed two days after her twentieth birthday at Copenhagen City Hall. They were a beautiful couple, the tall, distinguished man and the almost equally tall, young, beautiful girl. She was even a bit taller on the day because she wore stilettos under her wedding dress.

Adam had arranged for them to be picked up at the town hall by a limousine and taken straight back to the apartment. She did not want her parents to be present, and Adam's parents were no longer alive and he had no brothers or sisters. Neither of them had wanted to invite any other guests or go on a honeymoon. They just wanted to get married and have time to enjoy each other and all the pleasures in Copenhagen.

Hannah sank down on the soft seat of the luxurious car and looked at the marriage certificate they had just signed. She mumbled, "Now I have a whole new identity! Now I'm no longer Hannah Martins, but I've become Hannah Dahl. I wonder if that means I am now a full-grown frog?" She still clearly remembered all the many times as a child when she had walked around the big fountain and watched the frogs and dreamed of the day when she would develop from an egg to a full-grown frog.

But somewhere deep in her subconscious, she already knew that this was only the first step on her long journey. That she was not yet a fully formed frog but only a tadpole.

"I love your height." Adam kissed her affectionately. "You look amazing in stilettos."

Hannah gave him a loving pat on the butt. "I never thought I'd come to like being even taller than nature made me, but yes, I like the feeling of the high heels. You've taught me that it doesn't matter if the woman is taller than the man. I used to always duck and go in completely flat shoes or bare feet."

"The day you were brought into the hospital, and I saw you lying there in bed, with those long legs sticking out from under the covers, was one of the best days of my life." Adam was deeply serious. "That day, I knew you were something special. I knew I wanted to get to know you better."

"You're a good man, and I love you." Hannah kissed him long and deeply. She suddenly thought of something and let out a startled little fart. "Do you want to have children?" She wasn't sure if she could bear the thought of getting pregnant again and maybe losing the baby.

Adam shook his head. "Not necessarily. I'm perfectly content being married to you. But if you want to have children, then of course, we'll work it out."

Hannah shook her head. "I am not sure what I want. But perhaps..."

"Why not let nature take its course? If you get pregnant, then it's just great, and if not then we still have each other and our wonderful life together."

Hannah nodded slowly. It sounded reasonable.

Adam carried his bride into the bedroom and immediately started unbuttoning her dress.

It was the perfect day to begin a new life as a happy wife. Now Hannah had everything she could want. A man who loved her without dominating her. She enjoyed it to the fullest. Imagine being so lucky to have a wonderful man in her bed at night and during the day being able to paint and do whatever else she wanted to do.

Adam's expensive penthouse apartment in the new district of Copenhagen overlooking the canals was absolutely stunning. On its large roof terrace with space for sofas, sun loungers, a dining area, and a large barbecue, they often had guests, always couples, and always some of Adam's medical colleagues. Hannah had no friends of her own, but was perfectly content with the role of a beautiful young wife who was admired by his friends. A wife who was devoted to her husband, making sure he had a monthly haircut and delicious, often Italian, food on the table. "Today, we have guests coming over from the United States." Adam kissed his beautiful wife and smiled as she immediately let out a small burst of farts. "Aren't you going to wear those new shoes we bought last week?"

"You mean the pink stilettos with the towering heels and the silver buckles?"

Hannah had an extensive selection of cute shoes and boots and loved them all. Adam loved taking her into town to buy clothes and especially shoes. They spent a lot of time scouring the city finding new and exciting shops. He would happily spend hours looking for the right pair of stilettos or the perfect dress that would best accentuate her beautiful curves. She suddenly remembered the first pair of trousers she had had made back then on the farm. She vividly recalled her joy at finally having a pair of trousers long enough. But unfortunately, they burned up, just like her other belongings from that time. She grabbed a pink dress just recently bought and looked at herself in the large mirror that filled one bedroom wall and smiled. As a child and teenager, she never looked in the mirror, and while living at The Farm on The Edge of The World, she had no inclination to dress up at all. It was only recently that she suddenly realized how much she had changed. Virginia had started the process, but Adam had completed it.

Adam was so captivated by her looks and height that it affected her, and she began to like looking in a mirror. She had learned what the right clothes and makeup could do for her, and then, of course, there were the shoes. Adam wanted her to wear stilettos. At first, she'd thought it was utterly wrong, but now she'd grown fond of it and wouldn't do without them. Hannah wore high heels on occasions when she needed to look her best, but not every day. Makeup, perfume behind her ears, and then her feet in the pink stilettos—she made it just before the doorbell rang.

Adam loved it when his old friends and colleagues saw her for the first time. In high heels, she towered over the couple from America.

"So much beauty," the man said gallantly, shaking her hand. "You're a lucky man." He thumped Adam on the back, and Hannah could see that Adam appreciated the comment.

The little dark-haired doctor reminded her of someone she had once known. Hannah was just about to grab the thought when his wife held out her hand.

"Hi, I'm Charlotte."

Hannah smiled politely and took her hand. She was a pretty woman, not very tall, with short, cropped black hair and a slender body with small, almost invisible breasts. Suddenly Hannah remembered who the American doctor reminded her of. The doctor's hair grew in a funny spike at the nape of his neck, just like Henry's, the cute boy she kissed in sixth grade. She sighed and asked, "I once knew a nice boy called Henry. Your husband reminds me somewhat of him. Could it be a family connection?"

"I don't think we know anyone named Henry, at least not anyone who has ever been around Denmark," Charlotte replied.

Hannah sighed. What a pity. She would really have liked to meet Henry again.

"This is my first time in Denmark." Charlotte took a seat in one of the soft chairs on the terrace.

"It's nice and cozy here." Hannah already had a feeling that the slightly older American woman could become a good friend. There was something about Charlotte that reminded her a bit of Virginia. It was really strange, because on the outside, they looked nothing alike. But the way they looked at her was as if they saw *her* and not just a pretty young woman.

The two medical colleagues were already discussing the pros and cons of a particular method of treating burns.

"Do you have children?" Hannah asked Charlotte, taking a sip of the white wine.

Charlotte nodded. "Yes, two boys. They're staying with my parents for the next few weeks."

They chatted away, and time passed quickly, but Hannah did have periods in between when she lost the conversation because a cute little dark-haired boy poked his head out and brought back old memories.

"Goodbye and thank you. It was nice chatting with a person who understands what it's like to be a doctor's wife." Charlotte stood on tiptoe and gave Hannah a hug. "I hope to see you again some other time. You might even come to the States one day."

Hannah was about to reply, but Adam beat her to it. "We don't have any immediate plans to go that far away. We have plenty to do here." Adam wrapped his arms around Hannah's back and hugged her.

"I understand." Charlotte sighed and followed her husband out to the elevator. "But anyway, if things change, please come and visit us in Three Sisters. It's such a nice little town on the West Coast."

The West Coast! Hannah didn't want to be reminded of anything about the West Coast. Not even the West Coast in an entirely different country.

It was still too painful to think about the fire and Virginia. Hannah shut those thoughts out entirely and focused all her energy on her new life in Copenhagen. She sketched and painted often. Adam even arranged a room in the big apartment just for her.

Hannah could spend hours there while he was in the hospital. She forgot everything else when she was painting or sitting with her books and papers.

On a walk into town, Hannah had found an interesting shop, where there were handmade bags and other leather goods. A large, beautiful, shiny black leather briefcase with a code lock caught her eye from the window, and she entered the shop.

The black leather was silky and smooth. There would be plenty of room in the folder for papers and books, and the sturdy code lock would keep outsiders from her most private belongings. She had to own it. It was one of the few times she appreciated that she was equipped with a stack of credit cards and could buy whatever she wanted.

Hannah was usually very frugal, and expensive things didn't really interest her. Designer clothes meant nothing. But she had to admit to herself that it was finally nice to be able to buy clothes that suited her height. The shops had finally realized that there were actually many tall women. She didn't care about jewelry but loved shoes, and that gorgeous, soft leather briefcase.

She walked happily through the small streets, and when she reached Rundetårn, she decided to walk up there. She hadn't been there since she was a teenager. Before she met Anders.

Hannah gazed at the familiar view of the old part of Copenhagen's roofs and towers. She could see all the way across the park. The park with the giant rhododendron bushes where she had sat with Henry, that happy afternoon more than—she thought back—it had to be ten years ago. She had been twelve, and now she was twenty-two.

Something kept her from walking past the building where she had lived as a child. She hadn't been there since she was seventeen. And now that her parents were finally divorced and living elsewhere, she had no reason to visit that building that helped contain her isolation and sadness. Not even to herself did she admit that a childish kind of fear kept her from walking past her old apartment. It would have been an excellent idea to take that walk and get it out of her system instead of suppressing the unpleasant memories the apartment evoked.

Chapter 19

The river was wide and calm, but the water got murky and unclear, and the flat stones that offered respite were hard to see.

Hannah snuggled on the couch with her long legs resting in Adam's lap. Adam grinned and nuzzled his wife's thigh.

"The other day, I was reading an article written by a professor at one of the great universities in England. He wrote something about it being healthy to inhale anal gas!"

"Healthy?"

"Yes, he wrote that smelling small amounts of hydrogen sulfide could reduce the risk of blood clots, dementia, cancer, and heart attacks."

Hannah looked at her husband skeptically.

"That's true, studies have shown that. The professor also wrote that women's farts smell worse than men's. This is because women's farts have a higher concentration of sulfurous organic compounds that cause the smell."

"My farts NEVER smell!" Hannah tried to look innocent.

"You're not going to get me to sign that!" Adam grinned and continued, "And an average fart burns sixty-seven calories!"

"So that's why I'm so skinny." Hannah let out a tiny fart that barely had any odor and quickly kissed Adam before getting up to grab her notebook.

He continued, "And a person farts, on average, fourteen times a day!"

"That's hard to believe." She grinned and let out another small one.

"No, I think it's fourteen times ten!"

Adam reached out to her and continued, "Seven miles an hour is said to be the normal speed for a fart."

"Well, I can't comment on that, but we can try to measure it if the doctor can find a way to do it."

"I think we'll just leave that alone for now."

"The butthole is closed." Hannah sat on his lap and kissed him.

╱╌

Where had all those years gone? Looking back on all the many theatrical performances and dinners she had attended, either alone with Adam or with some of his colleagues, it seemed that it was always the external things that were emphasized.

Every year on their wedding day, she received the same gift, a beautiful piece of diamond jewelry. She opened her large jewelry box and laid the sparkling jewels in a long row on the dresser. One ... two ... three... Ten jewels, ten years.

She had asked Adam several times in the early years what he wanted, but he didn't like receiving presents. So instead, she made sure to dress up and make even more of their intimate moments on birthdays and wedding anniversaries. She sighed; lately, it had started to frustrate her that she found it so difficult to show her emotions. But she also knew that she was not yet done grieving and was not yet ready to let go. It reminded her of the time in the hospital, just after the fire, when she had met Adam for the first time. He had said something about how it could take many years before she was ready to start grieving and only when she was ready could she really let go of the past and become whole again. She was beginning to look forward to that day, when Adam's voice interrupted her wistful thoughts.

"Are you coming, darling?" Adam had a bottle of champagne in his hand. "Our guests have arrived, and we're just having a drink before dinner. I can't believe we're already celebrating our tenth wedding anniversary. These have been the best years of my life!"

"Mine too," Hannah replied automatically, allowing herself to be led into the living room. For a brief moment, she wished she were alone and could do as she pleased. Although it was nice to dress up, wear makeup, get her nails done, and everything else she did regularly, she missed the carefree days at The Farm on The Edge of The World when she would just throw on a pair of old pants and a T-shirt and walk along the beach in bare feet.

They didn't travel much. Hannah had often heard Adam say that there was no need to travel because he had everything he wanted in Copenhagen—his wife, his job, and his friends. Of course, Copenhagen was a great place to live, but once in a while it would have been nice to get away from it all and experience something new.

Hannah rarely enjoyed more than a single glass of wine with her meal, but her tablemates, some of Adam's colleagues, as usual, kept filling her glass, and Hannah's mood was well below zero, so for once, she got carried away and drank a lot more than usual.

As soon as they got back to the apartment, Adam took her hand and led her into the bedroom. He placed one hand on her breast and massaged it gently while he put the other hand between her legs. After more than ten years together, he knew her body inside out and how to satisfy her physically, and after a few minutes, she let out a little cry as her body contracted in an intense orgasm.

Happy and satisfied, he lay on top of her and finished quickly, well helped by Hannah's deft fingers in the area around his anus. A tiny fart escaped, but neither of them took the slightest notice of it.

The sexual relationship with Adam had finally taught Hannah what it meant to truly desire a man and be physically pleasured by him. But as the nights passed with their wealth of sensual pleasure, she realized she was holding back in a way in which he was unaware.

There was still a place inside her he couldn't reach. Something indefinable that made her yearn, almost painfully, for something to happen to her that would let her let go. Let go of all past experiences and feel free! No one was interested in her soul, her thoughts and dreams. Adam always paid for everything she wanted and he spent all his free time with her, so there wasn't really anything to complain about. She suddenly felt disgustingly ungrateful because she had started to dream of something else. Started to dream of something that Adam wasn't a part of.

Just before she drifted off to sleep, she thought that maybe that was how it was in all marriages. Once you knew each other and had been together for a while, it became routine and ... she searched for the right word—boring? It wasn't quite the right word, but she couldn't think of a better one. They were both sexually satisfied every time or almost every time. But something was missing.

If Virginia had only lived, she would have asked her advice. But *Virginia was no longer with her* and she had to find the answer herself.

Hannah knew that Adam loved her, and she felt that she loved him too. Could there be more degrees of loving? She didn't know, but no matter how hard she tried to convince herself otherwise, something was missing in their marriage. Something that was important to *her*, but something Adam didn't seem to miss. She pushed it away, for now, because she had finally persuaded Adam to go on holiday. A lovely holiday at the beach—not at the North Sea, but on the small, beautiful island of Bornholm—the easternmost part of Denmark and as far away from the North Sea as she could get.

※

Their vacation at the beach hotel on Bornholm had begun and Hannah was alert, her hair gathered in a ribbon at the nape of her neck, but a few curls had been let loose and stood like a halo around her face. They stood close together, and he had a hand around her slender back.

Adam smiled lovingly at her. He was so content. Suddenly she freed herself, untied the ribbon around her dark hair, let it fall freely, and laughed before carefully letting herself drift down the sandbank so that her skirt was pulled up around her waist, revealing her smooth brown legs. When she reached the shore, she looked up at him, a teasing glint in her eyes. "Your turn," she called out.

More sedately, even a little stiff-legged, he walked down to her and helped her to her feet again. He kissed her gently, but as usual, the kiss escalated and he did not release her until they were both heavily out of breath. Together they walked up towards the hotel. The holiday had begun.

Twilight crept in from the hotel garden and cast bluish-red shadows behind the sandbank. Like a thick velvet cloak, the evening muffled all sounds, quieting everything. The sea lay blank and black before them. Hannah felt entirely at one with nature. She had missed it, even all the mosquitoes and flies. She batted her hair, and the approaching insects flew a little way away before approaching the happy, fresh face again.

"Aren't you coming in soon?" Adam stood in the doorway of their room. "So many mosquitoes are coming in, and I can't stand the nasty creatures."

"I'll be in soon," Hannah promised, kicking off her shoes and running happily down the beach. Sand between her toes again felt great!

"Are you coming?" Adam tried to hide the impatience in his voice. But Hannah knew him too well. They'd been married for more than ten years already, and she knew perfectly well that he didn't like sand in his shoes and bugs and all the other unpleasantness you'd find in a hotel near the beach. Adam had only agreed to go on holiday there because it was something she wanted to do. A twinge of guilt came over her. He loved her so much that he rarely said no to her wishes.

"Yes, my love, I'm coming." Hannah sighed inwardly, grabbed her shoes, and walked up toward the hotel and Adam, who was still standing in the doorway waving away insects.

Lately, it happened more and more often that she experienced her day as one long Sunday, with nothing new or exciting happening—one of those Sunday afternoons when everything was closed, and there was nothing to do but sit and look at the sky.

"What are you thinking, my darling?" Hannah sat down on her tall husband's lap.

"I'm thinking about you," he replied gallantly.

As always, it was impossible to know what Adam was thinking, and as time went on, Hannah stopped asking.

It was strange now because she was married to a sweet and kind man, owned his love, didn't need money, didn't have to go to work, and had time to paint and read anything she wanted. She had no close friends, but several acquaintances she could call and go out with, but that wasn't what she wanted. What she really wanted, she didn't know, and therefore couldn't do anything about it. She had not yet realized that this was because her soul was not being stimulated and she was not growing as a person.

Back home after the holidays and ready for a nice dinner with a few of Adam's colleagues, Hannah looked at the place cards on the well-laid dining room table. Had it really become her identity to be Mrs. Senior Doctor Adam Dahl? She sighed and rearranged the flowers on the table. It was otherwise nice enough to have guests. Charlotte from America was so sweet, and Adam loved talking to her husband. But it was as if she had totally lost her own identity.

"Do you ever get lonely?" Charlotte looked at Hannah, who was in the kitchen making coffee.

She shook her head slowly. Lonely wasn't the right word for what she felt. Charlotte sighed fervently and accepted a cup of coffee. "Peter is always on the go. He never has time for me. His whole life consists of his job. His important job."

Hannah nodded in sympathy, fully aware that she was lucky to have such a kind and loving husband. Although Adam was also very busy at the hospital, he always had time for her. "Doesn't it help with the boys? You can't be too lonely."

"Yes, I'd give my life for those two youngsters, but I'm missing something. They don't make the loneliness go away. My heart is bursting with love when I look at them, but it's not enough. I don't know what to do." Charlotte looked at Hannah, took her hand, and asked, "Are you happy?"

"I never thought about that." But they both knew it wasn't true. She had known true happiness in those short months with Virginia. She had been happy there, a happiness that seeped into her innermost being and filled her whole soul. She was, of course, happy with Adam too, but in a different way. She couldn't quite put into words what the difference was, but she could clearly feel it.

"You don't seem unhappy." Charlotte smiled, a little enviously.

"What is happiness?" Hannah asked, half to herself.

"Do you ever feel lonely?"

"Yes," Hannah nodded. "I guess we all do from time to time. Loneliness has nothing to do with being surrounded by people. That's for sure." Hannah grabbed the coffee cups and prepared to enter the living room.

Charlotte sighed. "I never know what is going on in Peter's head. He's never been one to share his thoughts." She looked at her husband in the living room with Adam. "But men never do, it seems. Peter's just more closed off than most."

"Yes, it's really as if they hide everything inside."

Charlotte laughed, a slightly forced laugh. "It's the nature of the male. Sometimes I can't help but wonder if there is anything inside. Other than their work, of course."

Hannah knew there was far more to Adam than his work. But he wasn't good at talking about it. It was like Adam wouldn't allow problems to show up in his life. As head doctor, he wanted to have everything under control.

Adam joined them and embraced Hannah's shoulders affectionately. "It's time for a little supper on the terrace. Are you ready? I've already arranged the food, the delicious Italian food that you prepared earlier."

⁂

Hannah didn't even realize that after she married Adam, she got further and further away each year from what she once dreamed of doing and what she had promised Virginia. One year slipped into the next and it was clear that Adam had everything he wanted in his life.

If on some rare occasion she was in the mood to talk about the past and her violent experiences, he always tried to put it off and do something that would make her happy again. He obviously hated the fact that she had been surrounded by people who didn't love her and didn't treat her properly. For the same reason, they saw as little of her parents as possible. Adam had only visited her parents a few times, and they had been short visits. He quickly sensed that they were still not showing any interest in their daughter and he was quick to suggest to Hannah that they should do something fun instead.

Why don't we see what's playing at the theater tonight? Or take a ride in my new car. We could drive to that cozy little restaurant we found last year. Wouldn't that be nice?"

Hannah willingly followed and smiled when she thought about the attention they had attracted the week before when they had been in the theater. She was wearing her new red stilettos. Almost five inches extra to her six feet! More than six-and-a-half feet of feminine beauty, as Adam loved to put it.

The days at school and when she was young, when she bent her back to look smaller, were thankfully over. She loved the variety of reactions from people she didn't know.

But lately, she suddenly felt that something was missing in her life. Something was lurking in her brain. Something she'd forgotten. Something important. She closed her eyes and let her mind wander. Her body gradually relaxed, and her butt apparently relaxed too, for it emitted a long series of farts. Farts! Hannah opened her eyes.

Of course, now she knew what she was missing in her life. She had completely forgotten all about it in her busy, but rather superficial, life. It had been all too easy to forget that some people did not have the same opportunities as herself—to forget that there were people with problems and crises and sorrows and worries; tasks to be solved. It was time to start doing something about it. Hannah sighed deeply. After all, she had promised Virginia to keep studying and learning so she could one day help other people in need. Maybe it was time to buy a computer so she could keep track of all the notes she had lying around.

"Sorry," she muttered to herself. "I've been too busy with trivial things to do what I love the most. I have not fulfilled my promise to you, dear, beloved Virginia. I promise you once again that I will work hard and study and use my knowledge to help others."

When she had said the words aloud and repeated her promise to Virginia, Hannah felt as if a huge burden had been lifted from her shoulders. She straightened to her full height and shouted as loud as possible, "Swish swash, now I'm back on track!" She couldn't expect the technique she had once mastered to be at her disposal right away, but she had to study intensively again, and then she was sure it would all come back.

After that day, Hannah spent more and more time reading and soon felt that the words she was reading were making more sense. Just as Virginia had told her when she had dreamed of the maze and the many rooms of incomprehensible words. Hannah had never dreamed that dream since, but she felt sure that the next time it came to her, it would be because she could decipher the words on the walls of the many rooms and not just decipher them, but really understand the meaning of them.

"It's a sign of old age when you start to distrust youth, but fortunately, that'll never happen to me." Adam sat on the terrace and looked at his beautiful young wife.

"What do you mean?" Hannah lifted her eyes from the book she sat on her lap.

"As long as you're with me, I'll stay forever young," he said, feeling awkward, even after all these years, at the compliment.

Hannah always felt her heart swell with love when he complimented her, but this time she felt nothing. Even when he was buried deep inside her, she felt an emptiness. An emptiness that grew bigger and stronger every time they made love. A vacuum that made it hard for her to stay calm and lie still and let him love her. The last few times they had made love, she felt more like a spectator than a participant. And worse yet, a spectator who had not chosen to attend the performance herself.

For the first time, Hannah wondered if it might be time to try selling some of the things she had painted. Sell them so she could make some money of her own.

Chapter 20

The river was losing momentum, and it was time to escape from the stagnant, smelly water that was unhealthy to stay in.

Hannah now owned no less than seventeen different pieces of sparkling jewelry. Seventeen pieces of jewelry—seventeen years. They had been good years, but Hannah felt unsatisfied. Or rather, not happy, and to her inner ear, she heard Virginia say, "People almost always blame circumstances or conditions for what they are or are not, for what they have become or have NOT become. I don't believe in circumstances. The people who achieve their goals and become significant seek the circumstances they want, and if they don't find them, they create them themselves." Virginia's voice came through as clearly as if she stood beside her.

Hannah's phone suddenly began to ring, and she gasped. For a moment, she thought it was Virginia calling, but when she saw who it was, she was almost as stunned as if it had been Virginia who had found a way to contact her from the dead. She put down the phone and plopped down on the nearest chair.

Her father had called her to ask if he could visit. Hannah thought back to the last time she had seen her father. It must have been almost two years ago. Had she missed him? No, she had to be honest and say that she hadn't. Because how could one miss something one had never had? And she had never felt she had a father.

"Is something wrong?" Hannah poured a cup of coffee and handed it to her father.

"You have a beautiful place here." Her father ignored the question and looked out over the canal.

"Yes, we're thrilled to live here," she said. She looked thoughtfully at her father. The few times she had seen him over the last sixteen years, he had looked distracted and always busy doing a thousand things, never having time to listen or show interest in anything of hers. Something was very wrong.

"Are you sick?" That was her first thought.

He shook his head. "I'm thinking of quitting my job at the magazine..."

"Then you must be sick." Hannah sat down across from him and took his hands. "What's wrong?" He was younger than Adam, only fifty-nine, so he had many years left in the workforce.

"I'm not sick. I'm just getting tired of working so much." Her father looked over her shoulder, not wanting to meet her eyes.

Hannah considered for a second. Should she settle for the bland answer or keep asking until she got a response? "Will you please tell me what's wrong? I'm an adult now, thirty-six years old, and have been married for sixteen. I can bear to hear it."

Her father sighed deeply. "I've met someone."

"Well, there's nothing new in that. I believe you have a new lady every month."

"It's different this time." He looked away.

"Different, why?" There was something she hadn't entirely caught. She studied her father, noticing that he had lost some weight. He'd changed his clothes, too. They had become more casual. "Why is it different this time?" She repeated the question and smiled at him.

"It's not a woman this time."

"Not a woman?" Suddenly Hannah started laughing. She simply couldn't help herself. "After all these years of knowing hundreds of ladies, you discover you don't like women at all."

"Don't laugh. I'm dead serious."

"Yes, I can see that." Hannah looked at him and put her face in more severe folds. "So, you're telling me you've met a man?"

Her father nodded.

"A man you've fallen in love with?"

"Yes, he's the best thing that has ever happened to me. It's because of him that I've started turning my whole life around. It's because of him that I'm starting to realize how bad a father I've been and how many things I missed out on while you were growing up, and I was working all the time or running around with other ladies. I owe you an apology and if there is anything I can ever do for you, you know where to find me."

Long after she had kissed her father goodbye, Hannah remained sitting on the terrace, looking out over the city's rooftops. *Follow your heart wherever it takes you*, she muttered. That's how it should be. She was glad her father had found happiness. Something came to her mind. Did she love her father? She liked him, but she had to admit that she probably didn't love him. Not as it was right now, but love could come. And she held no grudge for the many years when he had been too busy to care for her. It had just been like that; it was in the past, and she couldn't change it. She wanted to face the future with an open mind, and if she got to see more of her father, it would be wonderful.

Adam lay in bed snoring. They had tried to have sex earlier, but Hannah had turned away when, after nearly an hour, he still hadn't gotten beyond fondling one of her breasts and wasn't responding to her desires or her caresses. It wasn't working for them anymore.

As his abilities dwindled, he became increasingly callous and impatient. Adam tried to give her an orgasm with his hand, but the more vigorously he tried, the harder he pinched her breasts and rubbed her clitoris, the more she resisted.

It was a slippery slope, and they both knew it.

Hannah came to think of a small shop in one of the old streets of Copenhagen. A shop that sold erotic toys. She clearly remembered a small handy black thing that had been in the window, along with a big sign. On the sign was a picture of a woman lying in bed with the black gadget between her legs. The woman seemed to be enjoying it. Maybe she should try to buy one of those?

She already knew that Adam wouldn't like that. He wanted to be the one to satisfy her. She sighed deeply, and after lying restless for an hour, tossing and turning, she got up again and slung a bathrobe around her before going outside to the dock. At that time of night, it was quiet, and the moon was shining, making a luminous path in the water. Hannah took off her bathrobe and adjusted her swimsuit before jumping into the sparkling crystal clear water. It was wonderful to live in the center of Copenhagen and still have the canals right outside the front door where one could swim in the night. She swam the breaststroke along the moon bridge, and only when she reached the other side of the channel did she turn around, change her swimming form, and lazily let herself slide on her back, looking up at the moon shining bright and golden.

She enjoyed the feel of the cool water against her skin. She swam until her muscles were tired, back and forth across the channel. Only when her breathing was no longer regular did she swim slowly to the ladder and hold on to it for a moment, regaining control of her breathing. She pushed the water off her hair before climbing the ladder and heading back to the dark apartment, and Adam, who was still snoring in bed and hadn't even noticed she'd been gone.

She lay beside him and clenched her hands so tightly that her nails pressed deep into her palms. She knew the night would pass endlessly with restless, burning tension throughout her body, alternating between wild rapture and sexual fantasies.

She sighed deeply and tentatively poked a finger down between her legs. After all, she had become accustomed to regular sex and satisfaction, so her body felt that something was missing.

The little pearl grew as her gentle rotating movements stimulated it, and suddenly she felt an orgasm coming a long way off. It was a very different orgasm from the one she usually had with Adam. This was a quiet and gentle contraction of her intimate area. A contraction as light as a butterfly's wing.

For a long time, she lay in bed with a finger pressed against her clitoris. Only when her fingers began to sleep did she move her hand and stand up to wash her hands.

At dawn, after a sleepless night, she suddenly succumbed to a violent crying fit. The tears had no acute cause, per se. But she had a need to get them out. And when she was done, she felt a peculiarly light heart, filled with indefinable well-being. However, it could always be seen for hours in the brown of her eyes when she had wept.

The sun hit her face, and she turned to face Adam. He was still asleep. He had been so tired lately. It wasn't like him at all. Usually, he was up early and doing his morning ritual. When his alarm clock went off, he would immediately get up and do five minutes of morning exercise before going to the bathroom, brushing his teeth, shaving, and putting on some aftershave before going back into the bedroom to give Hannah a warm and loving kiss. In the early years, that kiss was often the beginning of great sex, but in the last few years, it had often ended with the kiss.

She got up and walked into the living room to enjoy her usual morning impression—the sky over Copenhagen's broad main canal.

From the roof terrace, she could see well out over the water. But on the other side of the wide canal, the view was blocked by a row of tall buildings. When she blinked her eyes, she discovered, to her astonishment, that they were full of tears. For a split second, she allowed herself to think of the unlimited view there had been on the farm. At the farm, one could see across the deep blue sea to the end of the world.

Suddenly she missed the thrill of the speed down the river. The joy of not knowing where she would end up and what would happen.

She sighed even deeper than she had at night and went in to wake Adam.

"What time is it? I think I slept in." Adam looked at his wristwatch in wonder. "It's ... uh, it's ... I don't know..." There was a strange sound of astonishment in his voice. It was the first time Hannah had suspected that something was very wrong.

"You work too hard, my darling." Hannah took him by the shoulder and gave him a hug.

"My patients," he shook her off. "They expect me to be there for them."

"Yes, I understand that, but there are better ways to die than working too hard!"

Adam shuddered, blinked his eyes, and tried to focus.

"Luckily, today is Sunday, and you don't have to go to work. We're going to the theater tonight, but you can relax all day."

"That sounds good. So come down in bed with me so I can hold you." Hannah pulled her dress over her head and tucked herself under the duvet with her husband, lying quietly as he baited her like a little kitten.

～

Adam took Hannah's arm and guided her into the middle of the street as they exited the theater.

Hannah pulled herself free. "Stop! We have to walk on the sidewalk. We can't be walking around in the middle of the street."

Adam continued walking, a strange smile on his lips.

"Come on, Adam." Hannah stepped out and tried to pull him back onto the sidewalk.

A car approached, honking loudly, and Adam turned toward it, waving threateningly at the driver.

"Adam!" Hannah put her strength in, turned him around, and led him to safety. Something was definitely not right. This didn't seem like him at all. "What the hell got into you?" she asked, flustered.

Adam shook his head as if to clear his thoughts. "I don't know. I was sure I was walking on the little path behind the canal. I must be really tired."

There was something very wrong with him, and Hannah didn't know how to help. He was the doctor, for God's sake!

Deep down, Hannah already knew that what had just happened was the beginning of the end. She had no idea what the problem was but felt deep down that it was an unsolvable problem. It was also the end of *her* world.

Adam went to her. "You know I love you, don't you?" He tried to kiss her. "You know, even though I'm not very good at telling you?"

Hannah looked at him in surprise. "You tell me at least five times a day that you love me, so yes, I know, and I love you too." It was said without emotion, almost as if the words came from a machine. Hannah suddenly felt ashamed of herself. Why couldn't she love him more? After all, he was still the same sweet, kind man, even though there was obviously something very wrong with him. She adjusted herself to the fact that she was the one who had to make sure he got the help she already knew he needed.

"Just take it easy," Adam repeated for at least the twentieth time, without addressing anyone in particular.

⁓

Hannah woke up every two hours. Was he breathing? Was he okay? She glanced at her watch. It was only 3 a.m. and many hours until daylight. And what about when it got light? In reality, it wouldn't change a thing.

Adam was no different during the day than he was at night. He needed help. Professional help, and she wasn't up to the task.

He wasn't well, though he tried to dismiss it as just being tired. He passed out several times a day and was in a world of his own, a world where she couldn't reach him. He also had clear moments when he was still the sweet and kind man she had been with for almost seventeen years.

The recent turmoil gripped her as she put on her dress and stuck her feet into a pair of stilettos. She knew Adam loved her. She knew she was the woman in his life. She knew Adam would be angry with her when she interfered with his life and health, but she had to do something. There was no one else who could do it but her.

Surely, she knew the name of one of Adam's colleagues whom she could ask for advice? Over the years she had met many of them, and all the doctors had loved to talk about their work, which was perfectly understandable, but could become tiresome to an outsider. Hannah was sure that one of them had just been promoted to senior consultant in the dementia department. He was the one she needed to talk to. What was his name again? She closed her eyes and tried to see him in her mind's eye. Jonas—that was his name! At the same time, Hannah remembered that Jonas had tried to place his hand on her thigh during dinner the last time they had met. Well, never mind, she was a big girl. She could take care of herself. She needed to get help for her husband.

An inner voice said, *"Yes, if you want to take care..."* Hannah overruled the inner voice and found Adam's notebook in his jacket. It was time to find the number of the dementia specialist.

∕𝓏

Hannah could tell the exact moment when Jonas noticed her. He straightened his back and tightened his grip on the pen in his hand. Hannah didn't hesitate but walked straight up to him.

"Hi, Jonas," she said politely but almost coolly. He had an aura that affected her in a way she didn't want, and she had to be careful. *You must take charge*, a small voice in her head urged her.

"Shall we sit down?" Hannah didn't wait for an answer but sat on the chair opposite him and crossed her long legs. "I don't know how to begin, but something is very wrong..." She quickly recounted the incidents that had led her to suspect that Adam was becoming demented.

"Just leave Adam to me. I'll talk to him and sort it all out." Jonas rose slowly and approached her. She remained seated and looked at him.

"Do you remember what happened the last time we met?" Jonas held her gaze and placed his right hand on her thigh, the exact same spot as that time at dinner. He moved his hand a little higher up her thigh, still not releasing her gaze.

Hannah sat still, and a feeling of pure lust spread throughout her body. It had been so long since Adam had made love to her.

"I want to see you again," he said while slowly pulling away but maintaining eye contact.

༄

She would have finished early if her fingers weren't shaking so much that she had trouble buttoning all the little silver buttons on her dress. When she finally got all the way down, Hannah realized that she had buttoned crookedly, and she had to start over. She was unhappy with her appearance for the first time in many years.

Her tight-fitting brown dress revealed her beautiful figure, and the many small silver buttons were begging to be unbuttoned. She wore no jewelry other than large teardrop earrings that accentuated her long, beautiful neck. Hannah's brown eyes were wary as they studied him. She had agreed to meet Jonas. He had booked a table at a small, intimate restaurant on the outskirts of town. A place Hannah had never been.

Jonas looked deep into her eyes. "Let me make love to you. I'll give you an experience you'll never forget."

Hannah hesitated. She had never dreamed that she would cheat on Adam! It was not her style to do such a thing.

Jonas took her hand and placed it on his heart. "Feel it. My heart is beating just for you."

Hannah felt like she was standing in the middle of a hurricane and the high winds threatened to knock her over at any moment.

She tried to concentrate on the steak on the plate but her appetite had vanished.

"I respect you so much. You're so lovely." Jonas pulled her to her feet just after they had finished the main course and put an arm around her slender back, and together, they walked out into the night, out to his waiting car.

"Where are you taking me?"

"To my place." Jonas placed his hand on her thigh and squeezed it. "I need you, and you need me, so we'll both get what we want in a little while."

Was that really what she wanted? Hannah tried to get her thoughts under control, but it was impossible to think as his hand moved further and further up her burning crotch.

"Unzip my pants and take my cock in your hand. It's so big and stiff and ready for you." Jonas slowed and stopped the car in a deserted spot near the harbor.

Hannah came to her senses. What on earth was she doing? Having sex with Jonas wouldn't solve her problems; on the contrary! It would only cause her more of them—and worse. *Use your common sense*, Hannah grumbled to herself. Having sex with Jonas was not going to make her journey down the River of Life any easier, and it would hurt Adam unnecessarily.

She unfastened her seatbelt, but instead of pulling down his trousers, she opened the car door and got out.

"What the hell are you doing? Didn't I tell you to touch my cock?"

"Yes, you did, but I don't want to!" For a brief moment, Hannah felt like she was still a teenager, and Anders was bossing her around. But now, for God's sake, she was a grown, mature woman who didn't want to be bossed around. Those days were over!

"Won't? You can't fucking say that now. You've made me horny, and you'd better do something about it."

Hannah just looked at him and held his gaze.

"You know how much I care for you." Jonas tried to control his temper. "You're a lovely woman. I respect you so much and want it to be good for you too."

"Then prove it by treating me like a woman and not a thing. Prove it by being understanding."

"Understanding? You wanted this as much as I did. You were horny as hell and wanted cock. My cock! Not Adam's." Jonas' astonishment gave way to an anger every bit as fierce as hers.

Hannah took a step back as if he had struck her. "You understand nothing whatsoever."

"Yes, I understand perfectly. Such a bitch."

"You bastard. Get out of my sight." Hannah took off one shoe and pointed the stiletto heel straight at his face.

"With pleasure. I don't need a belligerent bitch like you anyway." Jonas slammed the car door behind him.

If you don't have sex with me when I want you to, I will destroy you. Then I'll tell Adam everything that's happened between us.

Hannah read the words Jonas had written for at least the twentieth time. That idiot! She had to have been fucking insane to even think of having sex with him. She almost ruined her marriage because of him.

At that moment, she realized that there was much more to it than that. She suddenly understood that the main reason her marriage wasn't working was that Adam still saw her as the young girl he was supposed to save or the beautiful young girl he was supposed to show off. It didn't seem like he wanted her to grow older and become more sensible. He was perfectly happy with things as they were, and so had she been … until recently.

Hannah looked once more at the paper on which Jonas had written his threat. That little piece of shit. What the hell did he think he was doing? She walked down the hospital corridor with quick steps, her stilettos clattering against the hard floor.

Where was he? The red lamp shone in front of his office. He was in a meeting. She didn't give a fuck. She tore the door open and entered the room.

Ten faces immediately turned to her—a furious young woman towering over them. What did that mean? There was curiosity in most of the faces. Jonas looked angry, and his fury did not diminish when Hannah walked up to his desk.

"Can't you see I'm in a meeting? Will you get out of here?" Jonas shouted, but fell silent when he saw Hannah's furious look. She stood behind his chair and tore up the paper, throwing the pieces into the air, so they descended like great white snowflakes over his head.

"I'm not for sale! I'm not your property or anyone else's. I belong to myself, and I have no intention of letting you decide whether or not I will have sex with you. We had dinner and *kissed*, and that was enough for me. I gave you one hour of my life, and you don't get another second of it. And just for the record, I will tell Adam what we did. Don't bother! And I'll find someone else to diagnose Adam."

With those words, she headed for the door. "I'll be off now, and you're nothing but a little piece of shit." She gave a good fart and disappeared out the door with her head held high.

～

Hannah sighed and turned in her sleep. The river ... she felt, she was heading back into the insidious and swift current. She whimpered and clenched her hands tightly around the pillow.

It was a difficult decision she had to make. One of those decisions that unfortunately came up in life—a decision that would make a loved one very sad, but a decision that was necessary for her in order to live a life that fulfilled her. She was so tired of being led around in the roaring waters. In her short months with Virginia, she had a rudder. She woke with a jolt and sat up, looking stiffly at the white wall opposite her bed.

A rudder!

She didn't have to look for a rudder. After all, she herself was the rudder! Why hadn't she thought of that a long time ago? She had to begin to use her common sense and believe in herself. She rose to her feet and looked at the big comfortable double bed she had shared with sweet, kind Adam for seventeen years. She'd had the best years of her life with him. The only thing that slightly comforted her was that Adam also had the best years of his life with her. A tear rolled down her cheek as she remembered his reaction when she had told him of her concern for his health and pleaded with him to get a diagnosis. It had been difficult to get Adam to see a doctor and he hadn't wanted her to go with him, so she didn't know the diagnosis unfortunately. It would have been good to know so that she could support him as much as possible. She sighed deeply. But her decision was made. Even though it hurt to leave a sick man, she knew she had to do it. Otherwise, she would feel like she was slowly dying.

She would tell Adam that she wanted a divorce, and she would be completely honest. That's the way it should be!

"This can't go on. We'll wear each other out. I want a divorce."

"You're ruining my life! I can't be alone! I can't live without you," Adam sobbed and hid his head at her breast like a little baby. Suddenly he turned his face to her, his lips quivering, and he wept. She would have preferred that he had scolded her, slammed the door, and gone away or kicked her out. After all, he had a right to be furious. She'd almost had sex with one of his colleagues. Hannah sat down opposite Adam and took his hands.

Chapter 21

The malodorous water disappeared beyond, and the water became clear again.

The rain continued steadily throughout the morning, bringing with it a coolness and a soft gray light that suited her current mood perfectly.

The rented room in one of Copenhagen's poorest and dirtiest neighborhoods was worn and bare, but quite large. The narrow bed did not take up much of the space, and it was the only piece of furniture except for a rickety wooden chair and a table that stood by the filthy window. The walls were whitewashed without a single picture.

Hannah sighed. Well, at least the lack of pictures on the walls was something she could quickly remedy. The double-stick tape had to be the solution. She looked at the paintings and drawings she had lined up against the wall. Her big black leather briefcase was there too. That briefcase contained all her notebooks, sketches, and above all, her computer—in fact, it was both her past and her future—everything she had worked on over the years.

She had made peace with Adam. She had promised to come and visit him as often as possible. She had told him the truth— that the years she had been married to him had been wonderfully good years, and that she would keep his surname and continue to be Hannah Dahl. Only for a brief moment had she considered taking back her maiden name. But she was not the same person she had been before her marriage, and therefore that name didn't suit her anymore.

She had kissed Adam goodbye and told him that she would always be deeply grateful to him, but she needed to find herself and figure out who she was when she was all alone. She then left her old life behind—the life she had lived for more than seventeen years. She had left a life where she didn't have to work and never lacked money. Now she had nothing except her personal belongings. Everything else she had left with Adam, except for a the jewelry she received as gifts on Christmas and birthdays, which she planned to sell to support herself until she could determine her next steps. She remembered Adam's saying and whispered to herself, *It will probably take many years before you are able to grieve and get the trauma from your childhood and youth out of your system.*

An urge to create suddenly rose in her with a force that surprised her. She felt a burgeoning excitement in her body as she grabbed a brush and focused on the large canvas. In her mind's eye, she saw in detail how the finished picture would look. What would be a good name for that picture? She did not hesitate but wrote with a firm hand on the back of the canvas: Soul Family.

She remembered Virginia's words: "A member of your soul family is a person you feel an intimate connection with from the first time you meet them." She had experienced it a few times. Her math teacher at the beginning of sixth grade, Henry, the sweet boy who gave her milk chocolate, and then her almost father-in-law, whom she had kissed when she was seventeen. That was nineteen years ago!

He had had a heart attack the day he heard that his only son had died in an accident and that his daughter-in-law had lost her unborn child. She had been informed of his heart attack when she was still in hospital recovering from the accident but hadn't been able to deal with it and had just repressed it as she used to. It was her fault that her farther-in-law had lost his son and grandson, and he must really hate her. But even if he hated her, didn't she have an obligation to do what she had put off for far too long? She couldn't neglect doing something just because it was difficult and unpleasant. It didn't suit her new self.

She thought to herself—*The person I am now is entirely different from the person I was then, and I will never be afraid again!* Hannah suddenly noticed that she was smiling—for the first time in weeks—for the first time since she'd left Adam.

She felt balanced! That was an amazing feeling, and she came to think of something.

What would Virginia say to her now? Hannah smiled again. She knew exactly what Virginia would say—*It's okay to get divorced, okay to break up with your boyfriend, okay to start over, okay to move on, okay to be alone. But it is not okay to stay with a person who does not fully support and value you. It is never okay to stay with a person who does not let you grow but holds you back because they are afraid that you will change and become someone different from who you once were.*

She had heard Virginia say that many times, but in recent years she had concentrated on Adam and his needs and had completely forgotten about herself.

Another of Virginia's teachings popped into her head—*Removing people from your life doesn't mean you hate them or don't care about them anymore. It just means that you take responsibility for yourself. If you don't learn the art of letting go, you lose yourself to the suffering of others, and that serves no one.*

Hannah suddenly felt that she had only just begun her life's journey. She felt that the previous years and their ups and downs had been necessary to provide her with the required knowledge and ballast to move forward as she was traveling from birth to death along her River of Life. She sighed and wrapped her arms around herself. She had been at the very bottom of the river, and she had felt as if she was flying on top of it. But she had never taken control herself. But the time was *now*. She felt a joy that penetrated her heart like a shining sun and filled her with a wonderful warmth. It was a feeling of having finally come to know her true self. She suddenly realized that she actually *liked* herself. For the first time ever, she really liked the person she saw when she looked in the mirror. She saw the real Hannah. Not a young insecure girl, not a scared teenager, not an adoring girl worshipping her mentor, nor a young woman being pampered by a loving and adoring mature man. She saw *Hannah*, a woman who possessed all human qualities, both good and bad; all the qualities that made her unique. As unique as everyone else was, and she promised herself that she would be true to who she was and always behave in a way that she could be proud of. Hannah sighed deeply. She was ashamed to discover that for so long she had repressed her own needs and desires and let her dreams vanish into thin air, suppressing everything Virginia had taught her and letting material things take over. She had lived a life of luxury that satisfied her body but not her soul!

She wondered what she was going to do. The answer came to her at once, and she said it out loud—*I want to work; I will no longer have to depend on others!*

Her father had offered to let her live with him and his new friend until she figured out what she wanted to do with her life, but she had said no. She knew she had to be alone and learn how to take control of her own life. The control that she had, so far, been unable to take but had pushed onto others—first Anders, then Virginia, and finally, Adam.

Dear lovely Virginia. Would she ever find out why she had visited her in the hospital that day? Why her and not just any other girl or boy who had been involved in an accident? There were so many unanswered questions and she regretted that she hadn't been brave enough to ask Virginia while she was alive.

She rose and stomped the floor in irritation. But the time had come to be brave. There were no easy answers anymore. It was time to act and behave like an adult and sensible woman of thirty-six, and not like a frightened teenager.

"I will earn everything I need myself!" she said out loud. "I earn my own money now!" She said it as if it was already reality.

The next question was how she was going to earn her money. For a long time, Hannah sat in the gathering twilight while hundreds of thoughts and possibilities flashed through her tired brain.

She had spent way too many years on the surface of the River of her Life. She had been skating across the water as if carried by invisible wings. Adam had tried to remove every problem for her. It was true that in the earlier years she had often found herself at the bottom of unpredictable waterfalls and had struggled to stay afloat. But that was no excuse to skate carefree through life now.

She suddenly remembered what Virginia had once said to her back when she was an insecure teenager on the way to New York.

Once you become SOMEBODY, you find your own way and become SOMETHING.

Back then, she had not been able to find her true self and become SOMEBODY. But even though her journey along the River of Life was not yet complete, she had learned enough to clarify what it would take to make her life fulfilling. For a long time, she sat with her eyes closed, listening to her subconscious. Suddenly, it pinged inside her head. She knew exactly what she wanted to do…

A pilgrimage! That had to be the answer. She suddenly realized that she actually wanted to know what happened to The Farm on The Edge of The World, where she had spent a few short but happy months. She gave it a second thought and corrected herself. Not just one pilgrimage, but several, as there were several people and places from the past that she needed to make peace with, both dead and alive.

To be continued in The River of Life 2

About the Author

Hanne is a Feminine Empowerment Expert, an Intimacy and Sexuality Educator, and she helps women feel sexy, confident, and empowered in all aspects of their lives.

Hanne wrote her first book twenty-five years ago (a crime novel). Since then, she has written seven books in different genres, all published in Denmark: personal development, women's fiction, and provocative romance.

In her upcoming book, *The River of Life*, she has mixed all three genres and written in English to ensure that the book will reach a much wider audience.

In her novels, Hanne mixes fiction with experiences from her own life, and it's always fun for readers to guess what's real and what's fiction!

Hanne is a Danish businesswoman and mother of three. She lives in a lovely apartment in a new part of Copenhagen overlooking the beautiful canals. She loves to travel, experience nature, and meet new people, and has traveled all over Europe and loves to drive around the US.

If you liked this book and would like to know how YOU can use YOUR common sense in a way that gives you an easier and more comfortable journey on YOUR river of life, take a look at:

hannebuggild.com

Here you'll find everything from FREE materials to a carefully customized program designed to help YOU let go of the past and make the journey on YOUR River of Life as fun and easy as possible. You'll learn how to use Common Sense in a slightly different way that creates amazing results.

Let your Common Sense guide YOU on YOUR journey on the River of Life and discover how to avoid the biggest waterfalls and dangerous whirlpools and have fun while getting the results you want.

Once you start using your common sense as a guide, you will be able to achieve impressive results.

Don't let the River rule your life - Take control!

Upcoming Book

Unlock Your True Potential

Unlock Your True Potential

USING A FEW SIMPLE METHODS

BUG Method

ZAP Method

WOW Method

HANNE BUGGILD

All the Methods you need to unlock your true potential and use your Common Sense in a slightly different way.

The BUG method - helps you let go of baggage from the past.
ZAP method - keeps you moving and prevents you from getting stuck.
The WOW Method - gives you self-understanding and makes it easy to identify your passion.

Read more on **hannebuggild.com**

The River Of Life 2 - Taking Control

Hannah finally takes control of her life and starts using her common sense to help others. She finds the answers to the mysteries of her past. But only after completing the exhausting Soul Walk, Virginia's most powerful tool. The Soul Walk that cost Virginia her life…

Read more on: hannebuggild.com

HEARTS to be HEARD

Giving a Voice to Creativity!

With every donation, a voice will be given to the creativity that lies within the hearts of our children living with diverse challenges.

By making this difference, children that may not have been given the opportunity to have their Heart Heard will have the freedom to create beautiful works of art and musical creations.

Donate by visiting

HeartstobeHeard.com

We thank you.

Made in the USA
Columbia, SC
19 June 2023